Leading, Teaching, and Learning the Common Core Standards

Leading, Teaching, and Learning the Common Core Standards

Rigorous Expectations for All Students

Rosemarye Taylor, Rebecca Watson,
and Joyce Nutta

ROWMAN & LITTLEFIELD
Lanham • Boulder • New York • London

Published by Rowman & Littlefield
A wholly owned subsidiary of The Rowman & Littlefield Publishing Group, Inc.
4501 Forbes Boulevard, Suite 200, Lanham, Maryland 20706
www.rowman.com

16 Carlisle Street, London W1D 3BT, United Kingdom

British Library Cataloguing in Publication Information Available

Library of Congress Cataloging-in-Publication Data

Taylor, Rosemarye, 1950–
Leading, teaching, and learning the common core standards : rigorous expectations for all students / Rosemarye Taylor, Rebecca Watson, and Joyce Nutta.
pages cm
Includes bibliographical references and index.
ISBN 978-1-4758-1027-1 (cloth : alk. paper)—ISBN 978-1-4758-1028-8 (pbk. : alk. paper)—ISBN 978-1-4758-1029-5 (electronic)
1. Education—Standards—United States—States. 2. Education—Curricula—Standards—United States—States. I. Watson, Rebecca, 1973– II. Nutta, Joyce W. III. Title.
LB3060.83.T39 2014
379.1'58—dc23
2014009968

♾™ The paper used in this publication meets the minimum requirements of American National Standard for Information Sciences Permanence of Paper for Printed Library Materials, ANSI/NISO Z39.48-1992.

Printed in the United States of America

Contents

List of Figures

List of Tables

Preface

It is the best time in contemporary history to demonstrate that public education in the United States can work well for all students. To respond to criticisms of public and private entities with positive student-learning outcome data, education professionals must commit to appropriate educator preparation, resources, and time needed to support diverse students' achievement on Common Core State Standards (CCSS). The authors believe that with implementation of the leading and teaching systems and strategies in this text, the percentage of US students achieving at high levels will increase.

Controversy surrounds the implementation of CCSS and related assessments. One of the issues is based on the belief that texts used in schools today have decreased in complexity during the last century. This belief has been challenged by Gamson, Lu, and Eckert (2013), who have examined 187 third-grade texts and 71 sixth-grade texts published as far back as the beginning of the twentieth century. The examination included two lexical difficulty measures, calculation of mean sentence length, and readability using the New Dale-Chall readability index. They concluded that text complexity has steadily increased since the 1950s for third grade, and for sixth-grade, text complexity has been stable since the 1940s. Keeping this finding in mind, along with the National Association of Educational Progress (NAEP) 2011 (US Department of Education, 2012) results of one-third of students in grades 3 and 4 read at proficient level and another one-third read below basic level, Gamson, Lu, and Eckert (2013) do not recommend that text complexity be increased in elementary school, but that instructional effectiveness be improved. Although text complexity is challenged as noted, text complexity is discussed in Chapter 4 as it relates to increasing rigorous expectations for students.

In addition to consistent implementation of effective systems and strategies for teaching and leading, improvement of students' engagement in learning is essential. Data gathered in the 2011 Trend in Mathematics and Science Study (TIMSS) suggests that student engagement is correlated to achievement (Robelen, 2013). In the study, students were asked about their teachers' actions related to engagement. Forty-eight percent of fourth graders said they liked mathematics, but only 26% of eighth graders indicated a positive attitude toward mathematics (Robelen, 2013). Similarly, 69% of the younger students indicated that they knew what their teachers expected them to do and that they are interested in what their teacher says. In contrast, only 39% of eighth-grade students responded that their teachers make efforts to relate instruction to their interests (Robelen, 2013). The students' perceptions of their engagement and teachers' efforts to engage them decline as the students move into middle school. Strategies to improve student engagement are addressed in this text through scaffolded instruction, clear goals, success criteria, and generative feedback.

The authors believe that CCSS controversies should be set aside to address solutions to the urgent need to improve leader and teacher effectiveness for enhanced student learning outcomes. The impact of teacher effectiveness on student achievement is undeniable. In addition to teacher-effect findings, there are less well-known principal-effect findings; in one year, a highly effective principal yields as much as two years and seven months' increase in learning, when compared to less effective principals (Branch, Hanushek, & Rivkin, 2013). For teachers' effectiveness to be maximized, principals, other leaders, and teachers need to own the same professional practices, high expectations, and commitment to all learners. Therefore, this text addresses the school professional community together to encourage transparent discussion and collaboration, to implement effective systems, and strategies grounded in research.

The CCSS movement has brought attention to rigor and expectations for all students to achieve at a national level of proficiency. As advocates for high expectations for historically under-resourced students, English learners, and those who perform below proficiency, the authors encourage education professionals to reset achievement expectations at the same level for all learners. In the authors' personal experiences and engagement with leaders and teachers who implemented the concepts within this text, results consistently have yielded improvements in teacher and leader effectiveness and gains in student achievement.

For many educators the implementation of CCSS has created a sense of urgency to develop expertise in specific research-based practices in leading and teaching. The authors believe that if the leading and teaching systems and strategies within this text are implemented with fidelity and consistency, there will be improvements in student-learning outcomes and success with

CCSS. By teachers, teacher leaders, and administrators having the collective expert knowledge and expert power that includes the same research and strategies with which to support each other's professional practice, student achievement will improve.

Acknowledgments

A book about how effective administrators and teachers can promote equity, excellence, and rigor for all students could not be written without outstanding examples of educators who embody these principles and achieve these goals. The in-context research we have conducted and presented in this book has been situated in schools of all types, but one quality is common to all sites—they are filled with dedicated professionals who believe in equity and access to excellence for every one of their students.

There are more teachers, administrators, instructional coaches, and other professionals than we can mention in this brief section, but we would like to single out a number by school name who have supported our work in very definite ways. We thank the teachers and administrators at Liberty Middle School, Ocoee Middle School, Stonewall Jackson Middle School, Celebration High School, Colonial High School, Oak Ridge High School, North Springs Charter High School, and elementary schools RCMA (Redlands Christian Migrant Association) Wimauma Academy, and the United Cerebral Palsy Bailes Campus Charter School. We are grateful to the outstanding educators in these schools for creating a culture of thoughtful practice in leading, learning, and teaching rigorous and effective standards-based instruction.

Beyond individual schools, there are many who have influenced our thinking, and we will recognize a few who have influenced this book in particular. We are indebted to our UCF colleague, Malcolm Butler, for introducing us to Henrietta Lacks, for influencing our thinking, providing examples, and for his excellent demonstration of Next Generation Science Standards (NGSS)–based instruction. Also, we appreciate the thoughtful teaching, practicing, and modeling of CCSS Mathematics by Edward Nolan, Director of Mathematics in Montgomery County Public Schools, Maryland.

Finally, we thank Amanda Ellis for modeling mentorship, leadership, and commitment to students and teachers at all levels.

Chapter One

Introduction

Leading, Teaching, and Learning the Common Core State Standards (CCSS): Rigorous Expectations for All Students is for those who believe in equity and access to excellence, to rigor, and to effective instruction for all students. Administrators, teacher leaders in and out of the classroom, instructional coaches, aspiring administrators, and teacher candidates will find thought-provoking insights and practical strategies for engaging diverse students and scaffolding them to success with CCSS. Readers can be confident that practices within this text are grounded in research, proven in schools and classrooms, and have promise for implementation across the United States in Pk–12 classrooms and schools. The CCSS are designed to guide curriculum development and organization of curriculum—not to direct instruction for teachers' use. *Leading, Teaching, Learning CCSS* offers effective practices for leading and teaching to improve students' learning.

Presented and explained are findings from in-context research on leading and teaching for higher student achievement. In working with many school districts, schools, administrators, and teachers, success in improving learning across all disciplines has been realized. Building upon and integrating each of the authors' specific areas of expertise, promising and proven teaching and leading strategies for student success with CCSS across grades and disciplines are shared. The intended result is that all students achieve proficiency as measured by CCSS and other respected assessments.

DEVELOPMENT OF COMMON CORE STATE STANDARDS

The Council of Chief State School Officers (CCSSO) were hindered in comparing one state's student achievement to another when each state had its own set of standards, used its own assessment to measure those standards (which often measured different skills or content), and set proficiency at varying levels. Furthermore, the National Assessment of Educational Progress (NAEP) identified only a 1% increase in eighth-grade students reading at or above basic from 1992 to 2011 (US Department of Education, 2012). When performance of students in the United States is compared to that of students internationally, they tend to be far from the top, such as 14th in the latest Program for International Student Assessment (PISA) (OECD, 2010).

These factors contributed to the conclusion by CCSSO that it was time for the accountability movement begun with No Child Left Behind Act of 2001 to become the national standards movement. CCSSO initiated the CCSS movement to respond to the call for increased student achievement in the United States. Today, 45 states have adopted CCSS all or in part. Standards are in English Language Arts (ELA) and Literacy in History/Social Studies, Science, and Career/Technical, and in Mathematical Practices and Mathematical Content. Standards are being developed for science and other subjects, but it is up to the states if these are to be adopted.

Previously, standards were set by individual states and usually based on those supported by professional organizations with broad representations, such as National Council of Teachers of English and the National Council of Teachers of Mathematics. With the majority of states adopting CCSS, there is an expectation of being able to compare student achievement nationally, rather than just within a state and having a common definition for proficiency (Common Core State Standards Initiative, 2010).

ASSESSING PROFICIENCY

There are two consortiums funded to develop assessments aligned with CCSS: Smarter Balanced Assessment Consortium (SBAC) (www.smarterbalanced.org/) and Partnership for Assessment of Readiness for College and Careers (PARCC) (www.PARCConline.org/). States have joined these consortiums confirming that they will use the assessments being developed beginning in the 2014–2015 school year. Educators across the country are keeping abreast of political decision making because as time has progressed, some state policymakers have decided to review decisions related to PARCC and Smarter Balanced and have considered other assessment alternatives, such as the ACT or to develop their own assessments. Florida and Georgia are two of these states that have withdrawn from one of the consortiums to make changes to the standards and assessment decisions. As an example, in Florida a standard has been added that reflects the need for students in grades 2–5 to learn cursive writing, as the state level leaders believe that cursive writing will assist in developing students' written communication.

Reading proficiency will be measured with a higher set of expectations than students have generally experienced prior to 2012. On grade level is considered to be proficient reading performance and can be measured by the Lexile Framework. The framework includes numerical ranges for readability of texts that are associated with grade level proficiency. As an example of the enhanced expectations, the reading Lexile range associated with each grade level has been raised:

- 725 as the upper Lexile in the range for grades 2–3 is now 790,
- 845 as upper Lexile in the range for grades 4–5 is now 980,
- 1010 as upper Lexile in the range for grades 6–8 is now 1155, and
- 1115 as the upper Lexile in the range for grades 9–10 is now 1305 (Hiebert & Mesmer, 2013).

These increases in what constitutes on grade level or proficiency in reading will impact the challenges teachers face in all disciplines; textbooks were already difficult for many students to read independently, particularly in science and social studies. Proficiency will be measured in reading informational and nonfiction texts in percentages larger than most state assessments and most state curriculums have required.

Performance tasks on the anticipated assessments being developed by PARCC and Smarter Balanced require reading more complex texts, more informational texts, thinking at higher levels and with greater cognitive complexity, and demonstrating their comprehension through writing (Calkins, Ehrenworth, & Lehman, 2012). While the expectations have increased from third grade through high school, here is an example of the kind of items third-grade students may encounter, to demonstrate that students must read closely. Similar to present assessments, third-grade students will be asked to read passages online and then select correct responses from choices that may include such skills as drawing conclusions and identifying word meanings from context clues. Additionally, for the same passage they may be instructed to drag supporting details into a graphic organizer. Subsequently, students may have a writing task that requires thinking across texts and completing such tasks as application of common experiences of the characters or the theme of the passages. As can be seen from this example, students will have to think more deeply about text than just to report recall or low-level comprehension knowledge.

Persistence will be needed for students to continue with items related to reading to which they may have to return more than once and respond with textual evidence from more than one passage. Teachers will be wise to increase the frequency of students' writing, particularly related to informational and nonfiction texts, along with the use of digital resources.

Although the sample items are well designed and seem reasonable upon review, there may be challenges in implementation. The assessments are electronic; students will need proficiency with using digital resources and will be more successful if they have access to appropriate digital resources at an optimal time of the school day during the assessment timeframe. During the testing window in 2013, the authors observed that students were taking digital assessments throughout the school day (beginning, middle, and end), rather than at optimal times due to the availability of digital resources which may have affected assessment outcomes. Another challenge is the expense of scoring written performance items. States may find the scoring expense and expenses related to appropriate digital resources in quantities for reasonable assessment timeframes to be overwhelming.

EMBRACE CCSS FOR STUDENTS' SUCCESS

Educators should embrace the opportunity to develop the best instructional approach for each unique context and discipline. Helping students to be more successful learners with CCSS will require educators to think differently than for achieving success on an assessment that focuses on recall or low- to moderate-level thinking and cognitive complexity items. For students to be successful with moderate- to high-level thinking and complexity items, teachers must master the academic language and concepts prior to helping students to learn them.

An example of supporting teachers' knowledge development for success is Pinellas County School District, Florida, which implemented CCSS in primary grades during 2013. These primary-grades teachers participated in intense professional learning related to deep understanding of CCSS for Mathematical Practice and Mathematical Content. Developing deeper and accurate understanding of mathematics is essential so teachers do not rely on the textbooks only or on tricks of computation, which do not serve students well in higher levels of mathematics.

The CCSS help to integrate instruction across disciplines and should be used by all teachers to increase learning, regardless of teaching assignment. Emphasis on thinking at higher levels and completing more complex learning tasks is part of the integration of content. In science, students use mathematics and English language arts as they show their data in tables, and write their hypotheses and conclusions. Problem solving and drawing inferences is applicable to mathematics, science, English language arts, social studies, and electives (arts, career/technical, health/fitness, world languages).

As leaders provide for collaborative planning and reflection, teachers will see the connections across disciplines and how each teacher supports the other's success through the use of literacy processes of reading, writing, speaking, listening, and thinking. Readers may find example modules developed by teachers in varying disciplines and grades in the Literacy Design Collaborative (literacydesigncollaborative.org) that address learning tasks aligned with CCSS to be helpful.

ORGANIZATION OF LEADING, TEACHING, LEARNING CCSS

Increasing the frequency and quality of the thoughtful practice of leading and teaching rigorous and effective standards-based instruction is the purpose of this text. Each chapter begins with the topic focus and then provides an analysis of the specific focus (research-based instruction, nonproficient readers, etc.). Examples within the chapters address kindergarten through high-school students and various disciplines. Digital resources are infused as appropriate, along with challenges that may arise. Chapters end with Practical Steps for Leaders, Practical Steps for Teachers, and Useful Academic Language. It is hoped that the reader will have a better understanding of the challenges before them and solutions that promise success for all students as strategies for leading, teaching, and learning CCSS are mastered.

Teachers and leaders have to think differently about instruction and classroom assessments. Chapter 2 addresses research based instruction and scaffolding students' learning to independent performance. These are changes in professional practice for leaders and teachers to think about as they enhance instructional effectiveness. Expectations of the CCSS are demonstrated independently, requiring teachers to scaffold students to independence and not end instructional experiences in guided practice or collaborative groups, as has become common in many schools.

Focus on academic language will be essential for students to understand and demonstrate the thinking required (Chapter 3). Science, mathematics, and social studies teachers know that the roadblock to accessing their disciplines is often the lack of academic vocabulary and accurate background knowledge. The CCSS present the mastery of and modeling of accurate academic language as imperative for all teachers and administrators. Accurate use of academic language aligns with uncovering students' misconceptions that hinder their advancements in learning, particularly in mathematics, science, and social studies.

Integration of disciplines and asking students to provide textual evidence for their oral and written responses will be essential. There is no room for guessing in classrooms, but for inferences, conclusions, and conjectures supported by evidence both literal and implied. Analysis is expected to take place across several texts, each of which may be shorter than the longer single works traditionally read. The level of rigor in the expectations for performance is not only a higher reading Lexile range to be proficient, but also demonstration of more high-level and complex thinking across texts, which is discussed more in depth in Chapter 4.

Chapters 5 and 6 address unique instructional considerations and strategies to support student mastery of CCSS of English learners (ELs) and under-resourced students. For these students, CCSS will be particularly challenging. However, effective strategies and decision making specific to these groups of students and that also work well for others will be shared.

Finally, Chapter 8 focuses on building capacity for continued learning and increases in teacher effectiveness and leader effectiveness resulting in better student-learning outcomes. The intent is for teachers and administrators to have confidence in their analyses leading to instructional decision making and practice that are grounded in evidence and research.

PRACTICAL STEPS FOR LEADERS

- Make a plan for acquisition and development of expertise with digital resources by faculty, staff, and students.
- Support teachers in adjusting instructional expectations of students.
- Communicate with families on how the anticipated changes in expectations will assist students' success through K–12 school and in their readiness for careers and college.
- Seek out vetted online resources for leader and teacher use such as:

  - Navigating Text Complexity: www.ccsso.org/Navigating_Text_/Complexity.html
  - Working With Diverse Learners: http://ell.stanford.edu/
  - Universal Design for Learning: www.cast.org/learningtools.index.html
  - In Common: Writing for All Students: www.reading.org/achievethecore (DiGisi, Parker, & Shaw, 2013)

PRACTICAL STEPS FOR TEACHERS

- Become familiar with the CCSS.
- Review the consortiums' websites and resources for teaching and for families. (www.smarterbalanced.org/; www.PARCConline.org/).
- Become familiar with the consortiums' sample assessment items and regularly include the models in instruction.
- Model the use of academic language with students and colleagues.

- Be sure to move students to independent practice after success in collaborative learning.

USEFUL ACADEMIC LANGUAGE

Evidence—Facts, figures, details, quotations, or other sources of data and information that provide support for claims or an analysis and that can be evaluated by others (Common Core State Standards Initiative, 2010, p. 42).

Independent—Student performance without scaffolding or support from a teacher, other adult, or peer (Common Core State Standards Initiative, 2010, p. 42).

Lexile Framework—A system of numerical ranges for readability of texts that is associated with grade-level proficiency.

Performance tasks—Items or questions provided to students on which they are to demonstrate mastery of a concept or skill (Common Core State Standards Initiative, 2010).

Proficient—Successful independent student performance with on-grade-level text or expectations.

Chapter Two

Effective Research-based Instruction

When planning for effective instruction, teachers should begin with clarifying the intention of the learning (Hattie, 2009), which typically is a benchmark or Common Core State Standards (CCSS) that drives the curriculum. Thinking about the success criteria or what achieving the benchmark would look like should be the next step (Hattie, 2009). Until the teacher is very clear on the learning outcome expected and has a model or example of the expected learning outcome to share with students, the remainder of the instructional planning should be delayed. Clarity in students' minds on the expectation is essential. Otherwise, the result of the teacher's and students' expended time and energy will not meet expectations.

Teach, model, and practice—don't just assign work. This mantra helps teachers in all grade levels and disciplines to think about how they plan instruction as a scaffolded learning experience that moves from high to low support as students become more proficient within a lesson and within an instructional unit. It is helpful if teachers conceptualize their teaching as interactive learning with responsibilities on the part of the teacher and students. Effective instruction is not represented when the teacher tells the students information and then the students try to complete an assignment independently, often with lack of success, frustrating both students and the teacher.

The authors have found that the majority of teachers do not take the time in their instructional planning to think about the steps involved to scaffold students from high support to low support or independence while carefully intervening and differentiating instructional support to individuals and groups of students. Time invested in planning details of instruction saves time during the learning experience and enhances student success. An easy to use resource that teachers may find helpful in instructional planning is *The*

Lesson Planning Handbook: Essential Strategies that Inspire Student Thinking and Learning (Brunn, 2010). If the school is focused on CCSS instructional planning, teachers and leaders will find helpful modules across disciplines and grades on the Literacy Collaborative website (www. literacydesigncollaborative.org/).

Leaders are encouraged to collaborate with their faculty and staff on the best approach or model for effective teaching that leads to improved learning. In that model it is helpful if there are nonnegotiable expectations for instruction, such as teachers scaffold instruction, assist students in acquiring vocabulary and academic language with research-based strategies, or include moderate- to high-level thinking and complexity items (Taylor, 2007; Taylor & Gunter, 2006). In addition to these examples, The Literacy Leadership Team (LLT) at Oak Ridge High School (ORHS) in Orlando, which has representatives of all disciplines, developed other nonnegotiable expectations for themselves and colleagues across all disciplines.

1. Consistently teach, model, and practice student-owned literacy strategies with evidence to foster independent success: predication, clarification, visualization, asking questions, making connections, summarization/synthesis, and evaluation.
2. Implement ORHS Instructional Release Model appropriate to the discipline. (Figure 2.2)
3. Support improvement in writing through application of the ORHS Writing Rubric.
4. Engage students in learning with digital resources. (Oak Ridge High School Literacy System, 2013, p. 1)

The reader can see that these expectations reflect the CCSS. Given that these nonnegotiable expectations were developed by peers and recommended to the principal, there is an expectation that the implementation across the school will assist in success with CCSS. Leaders in schools and school districts may want to consider a similar approach in achieving commitment to higher expectations.

SCAFFOLD INSTRUCTION

There are various models that can be used to begin instruction with high support and as students demonstrate success, remove the scaffolds of support. Two models are shared in this section: one developed by the author and one developed by teachers. Both models have as the foundations the lesson design of Hunter (1984) and Marzano (2007).

Lesson Introduction

The benchmark or learning task introduction serves to create interest and to engage students in the learning experiences that follow. It is the time to carefully access and develop background knowledge necessary for success on a given learning target or benchmark. Even when students are grouped according to an achievement measure, their background knowledge and skills vary based on the effectiveness of previous teachers, family and personal experiences, and interests, which drive deeper levels of proficiency. In the urban school community in which the authors live, there are numbers of students with gaps in their learning due to lack of available schools or natural disasters (e.g., Haiti's earthquake), making access and teaching of background knowledge essential before directly instructing a new benchmark. Chapter 6 will address some of these differences that affect students' background knowledge and readiness to learn specific content and skills.

If the reader reviews Figure 2.1, the original of which was published in *Leading Learning: Change Student Achievement Today!* (Taylor, 2010, p. 103) it can be seen that before moving to developing proficiency, students need correct background knowledge that is void of misconceptions. Discovering misconceptions is an important part of developing accurate background knowledge. For example, is the side of the moon we cannot see the dark side of the moon or the back side of the moon? Do students know the difference among science fiction, pseudoscience, and science related to a specific standard, benchmark, or learning task? One way to identify and clarify common misconceptions is to list a few facts and misconceptions, followed by asking the students to select those they believe to be true, and for those they believe to be misconceptions rewrite the statements to be accurate. Another easy strategy is to have a quick write at the beginning of instruction and ask students to bullet three things they believe they know about the topic to be studied; then address the misconceptions and confirm accurate items.

During this phase of learning the teacher should build a mental model of what is to be learned while using academic language and introducing key vocabulary. (See Chapter 3, Academic Language.) Through the use of visuals, video streaming, online resources, and shared practice (students and teacher working together at the same time) students can build basic understanding of the learning target upon which to ground the intended learning (Glenberg & Kaschak, 2002). Another simple, but effective strategy that can be used for those without digital resources is a text feature (maps, charts, graphs, headings) walkthrough of a chapter or passage while introducing essential vocabulary. As students cognitively walk through the chapter they will infer from the text features and generate questions or "I wonders" related to visuals, maps, and charts.

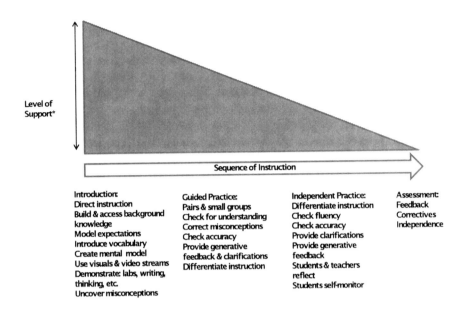

Figure 2.1.   Scaffold Instruction Model. Created by Rosemarye Taylor.

A geography teacher begins each unit on a continent, with students identifying geographic features (rivers, deserts, mountains, etc.) and hypothesizing how these may influence the lives of the peoples who inhabit the region. The text headings provide other clues to assist students in generating hypotheses to generate interest, building background knowledge, and academic language. A typical student's hypothesis might be,

> "There is mostly desert and just a few water ways in this region so it must be hot. I think the people would dress to be cool, stay inside during the middle of the day, and their houses would be as cool as possible. I don't think they farm much."

These strategies can be used in any discipline to access students' background knowledge and to build essential knowledge upon which to ground the unit's instruction.

- Modeling of the success criteria by the teacher should also take place during this time. What does a well-written sentence or paragraph look like and what makes it well written?
- Which strategies should I consider to solve this problem? How will I solve it and explain my answer?
- How do I explain the steps I took to find this solution?

By the teacher sharing the practice and thinking used in writing the paragraph, working a problem, or explaining a solution with students, they have high support with success prior to moving to guided practice with less support to collaboratively practice the same learning task. Students listen, watch, and participate with the teacher; they do not just listen.

Guided Practice

The next phase of learning is guided practice during which students are collaborating on their learning task. Purposeful and deliberate practice of correct academic language is essential for students to improve reading and writing in any discipline. Guided practice is a good time for oral language development practice, keeping in mind that development of students' oral language is related to development of their reading comprehension and writing. For collaboration, students may be in pairs, triads, or quads—but more than four students would be too many for all to participate.

During guided practice each student needs a role or should have a responsibility for an outcome. In working a mathematics problem teachers may have quads of students follow this procedure: With support from the others Student 1 completes step 1, Student 2 completes step 2, Student 3 completes step 3, and Student 4 explains the steps. The teacher would provide feedback to each group as they worked and perhaps to the class before students would begin the next problem. The second problem would begin with Student 2 completing step 1, and Student 3 completing step 2, and so on. After the completion of four problems in guided practice, each student has had moderate support to work the entire problem type and gotten feedback on each step. Working one step with help from peers is less difficult than working an entire problem alone and builds confidence. A similar process could be used with pairs or triads and with any discipline as deemed appropriate for the grade level and students' proficiencies.

Teachers may organize the room in groups that facilitate learning while providing for smooth routines. An excellent practice is to have the model of the expected work in the center of the room. One member of a group at a time may go to the model and see what the next step is or compare the group's work to determine how to improve upon it.

In a geometry class visited, the teacher had four tables, each in a quadrant of the room. The students were to assist each other and one representative at a time could approach the teacher's work station with a question or clarification needed. When teams work to find solutions and solve problems in any discipline, learning is anchored for deeper learning to take place over time (Bransford, Brown, & Cocking, 2002). Routines such as these facilitate effective guided practice that is purposeful and deliberate.

Guided practice is the step that we have observed to be most often skipped in middle- and high-school classrooms. Many teachers do not think it is necessary as they believe that their curriculum or focus calendar demands an intense pace. Classroom management and keeping students focused on the task at hand is another reason teachers give for not implementing guided practice. A middle-school social studies teacher said, "I keep students in whole class instruction because they get off task if I ask them to work in pairs." To reduce off-task behavior the students must have successfully practiced the task in shared instruction. Additionally, short, specific timeframes for the guided practice are important so that they do not have time to do anything but the task at hand. An instructional practice that works well might be like this, "Students, you have three minutes for the pair work. Please watch the time on the interactive board." As the teacher checks for understanding during this time, she may add another minute or so depending upon the progress students make.

In summary, guided practice is the instructional component during which students build endurance and confidence. Once they have demonstrated mastery or proficiency in the target learning, it is time to move to independent practice. Well-planned guided practice assists students in readiness to complete work accurately in independent practice and is essential for increased percentages of students to independently demonstrate proficiency.

Independent Practice

As students experience success and accuracy is checked and confirmed by the teacher, then it is time to move to independent practice. If some students are ready for independent practice and others are not, then independent practice is a good time for the teacher to work with a small group of students who need extra support, just as she would have done during guided practice. Students should only practice independently when they have demonstrated 90% accuracy on the learning task in guided practice.

Independent practice may be homework in addition to class work. It is not suggested to give homework on a skill or concept until students have demonstrated success in class by themselves to avoid practicing incorrectly. Homework should not be dependent upon the student having a resource within the home environment.

There are well-meaning teachers who believe that collaborative groups are important to the point that independent practice is not necessary. This is a misconception as students are held accountable, as are teachers, based on students' independent demonstration of proficiency on assessments. These assessments include teacher-made quizzes and tests, accountability assessments, end-of-course assessments (within a school, school district, or state), or with CCSS.

As students practice, they overlearn to automaticity, and the learning moves to long-term memory. Inaccurate practice moves incorrect learning to long-term memory, which is very difficult to unlearn. Therefore, students must practice correctly.

We call incorrect overlearning the Tim Tebow effect. Readers may not know Tim Tebow, so here is shared a little about him. As an elementary- and middle-school student he played football. His coaches and family practiced with him over and over until he was the best football quarterback in his home town. This acknowledged skill made him successful in high-school football and he was recruited to the University of Florida and became a star quarterback. As might be imagined, he was so successful that he was recruited to play professional football as a quarterback.

Unfortunately, Tim had learned to pass a football the way some describe throwing a softball. His passing method had worked well for him for 15 years, but when the proficiency (accuracy and rate) bar was raised to the level needed in professional football he had to unlearn the way he passed the football and learn a new way—which was almost impossible. It is too soon to know exactly how overlearning the incorrect pass technique for football will end for Tim, but it is thought that his knowledge of the game might be better used as a sports moderator.

For students in your schools, it is very important that they do not experience the Tim Tebow effect of overlearning incorrect disciplinary language, content, or skills, which will be almost impossible to overcome. Independent practice must follow success in guided practice.

Assessment

After success in independent practice, it is time for assessment, generative feedback (Puig & Froelich, 2011), and linking this learning task to the next standard, benchmark, or learning task. If students are not successful in guided practice, the teacher should provide another model or explanation; if students are not successful in independent practice, more instruction and guided practice are called for—not a repeat of the same strategies or more practice.

In addition to the Scaffold Instruction model found in Figure 2.1, included is Figure 2.2: Oak Ridge High School's Instructional Release Model. This model was designed by the high school's LLT. After studying models of instruction (Taylor, 2007; Fisher & Frey, 2008; Marzano, 2007; Hunter, 1984), the LLT designed this model that emphasizes shared practice prior to guided practice, the student's responsibility, and examples of instructional strategies that teachers may select to use. The LLT was empowered by the principal to design the ORHS Instructional Release Model and it has become the expectation for all teachers within the school to use.

Sample Science Instructional Plan

A first-year teacher developed an instructional plan with components of scaffolded instruction. Excerpts follow that represent the essential question (big idea), learning goal/target for the day and benchmark that extends over several days. Please note that the benchmark verbs of *apply and interpret* are aligned with the success criteria of the instructional plan's components, such as "apply" takes place in the lab and "interpret" takes place as students write the report using evidence from the lab experience.

> Essential question: Why does it take more force to make large objects accelerate as much as small objects?
> Learning goal for today: Students will understand the relationship between net force, mass, and acceleration known as Newton's Second Law.
> Benchmark for the topic: Interpret and apply Newton's three laws of motion.
> Introduction: The teacher introduced Newton's Second Law, using visuals and demonstrations.
> Guided practice: Students collaboratively applied Newton's Second Law in the lab. The teacher circulated, assisted, and provided individual attention particularly to ELs. Differentiation was provided by a rewritten lab guide in simple but accurate language for the ELs to follow, along with the individual more intense support.

Process	Teacher	Student
I do (interactive practice)	Models: provides direct instruction, activates prior knowledge & cognitive engagement, provides think-alouds	Connects: thinks, engages, takes notes, asks & answers questions, listens
We do (shared practice)	Leads: demonstrates, probes, explains, clarifies, provides feedback/generative responses	Responds Actively: puts forth effort, collaborates in whole group, listens, thinks
We all do (guided practice)	Facilitates: evaluates, encourage, clarifies, provides feedback, corrects misconceptions, differentiates instruction	Applies Learning: collaborates (groups, pairs, etc.), clarifies, practices
You do (independent practice)	Monitors: assists, provides feedback, differentiates instruction	Develops Ownership: self-monitors progress, develops mastery/independence

Figure 2.2. Oak Ridge High School Instructional Release Model. Created by Oak Ridge High School LLT with permission from Leigh Ann Bradshaw.

Independent Practice: For the lab report, students were given probing questions to think about, rather than only to report the steps taken during the lab. The outcome was their interpretation of Newton's Second Law supported by evidence from observations in the lab.

ENGAGEMENT

Engagement means that a student is thinking or cognitively engaged in the learning. At the lesson introduction it may be referred to as the hook, meaning to hook students' interest. He may be doing a variety of learning processes such as listening, speaking, reading, writing, solving a problem, or participating in a lab. It does not mean that students are having a hands-on activity only. If you review the ORHS Instructional Release Model you will see that the teachers identified providing for engagement as something the teacher does, but the students are to engage by listening, thinking, asking and answering questions, collaborating, clarifying, and monitoring their learning. Students are not passive recipients of learning, but actively doing the work of learning.

Since many of the engagement processes are invisible, how will the teacher know if the student is engaged? If a teacher or administrator scans the classroom, he may see students who look as if they are working, when in fact, the work may be incorrect, or they may just look like they are working. To determine if students are engaged, speak to students, look at their work, ask questions, and listen to them. Do they know what they are doing, why they are doing the work, and is it being done correctly?

When visiting classrooms, the author asks students to tell what they are doing. It is not uncommon for a student who is off task or does not understand the work to suggest that the author ask the teacher or say "I don't know." Here is an example from a primary classroom in which the first-grade student knew what she was doing and why, and used academic language to explain.

"Tell me what you are doing today." (Author)

"I am in the listening center working on my fluency." (Student)

"Tell me what fluency means." (Author)

"Fluency means reading like you speak." (Student)

When visiting a social studies class in a high poverty school, the author saw students working in collaborative groups and using their iPads. The author asked one group what they were doing as it looked like they were playing.

"Help me understand what you all are doing." (Author)

"We're playing jeopardy to review vocabulary. Want to try?" (Student)

"Thank you, would you mind if I watch?" (Author)

"See, (demonstrating) you can photograph the words you need to study, and make flash cards." (Student)

The students were engaged with studying vocabulary in this social studies class and not just engaged with the device—which teachers should monitor closely.

TEACHER-LED SMALL-GROUP INSTRUCTION

Collaboration in small groups has been mentioned as appropriate for guided practice. Some schools require teacher-led small-group instruction for all students as a way to provide more personal attention to students, particularly in literacy. However, this practice is appropriate in all disciplines and grade levels. These groups may be heterogeneous or may be organized by student skill or knowledge development needs dependent upon the students, discipline, and resources. Small groups should be flexible and change in student composition based on evidence of their learning to avoid negatively labeling students.

Teacher-led small-group instruction can be effective for intervening during guided and independent practice in any discipline. This is a way to differentiate with intensity or student-to-teacher ratio whether students lack proficiency or have mastered the learning target and need to go more deeply into the topic. The authors suggest that the same benchmark or learning target be expected for all students when the teacher-led small-group instruction is used as intervention. Differentiation can be in time, intensity, or instructional resources, but not in expectations.

As teachers gather evidence in the classroom on students' learning, they know who is learning and at what pace on a particular benchmark or learning target. A quick review of students' work allows the teacher to know who needs additional assistance and with what specific part of the expectation. She can ask for no more than five students to join her at a desk or kidney table to assist as they work on the learning task, to provide correctives for misconceptions, and generative feedback (Puig & Froelich, 2011). Small-group instruction is not the same instruction repeated, but specific to these students after gathering evidence, which again is providing students with more time, intensity, or perhaps additional resources. These small groups do not always have the same students, but change as the learning targets change.

They do not take place each day, but as needed for as little as 5 to 10 minutes. The same concept applies to an individual student with unique learning needs who benefits from intense assistance in terms of time or different instructional resources to master a particular concept or skill.

Teacher-led small-group instruction may also be used for instructional differentiation during a time when other students work independently or collaboratively at stations or learning centers, sometimes called rotations. Stations or learning centers are for practice after students have been successful in the whole class and guided-practice learning experience. All students may go to each station or students may be asked to work at specific stations to differentiate practice based on evidence of their learning. Certain instructional programs include digital resources that adjust to each student's independent reading level; these may also be a station.

Effective stations are for practice on important concepts or skills or may go more deeply in learning as is recommended for proficient students. They are not for introduction of new skills or content. Nonproficient students need more practice with frequent feedback and proficient students should learn the concept more deeply by reading, thinking, writing, seeking solutions, or otherwise working at higher levels of thinking (Koedinger, Corbett, & Perfetti, 2012). Each station should be clearly labeled with instructions and a model of the expected work to support independently achieving the expectation. Students should be given feedback on tasks completed just as they would with any work product. Classroom procedures are important for effective centers or stations so that transitions to and from them takes less than 1 minute.

CHECKING FOR UNDERSTANDING

Hunter (1984) was one of the first to advocate for frequent checks for understanding. The purpose is to teach in small chunks to assure understanding and accuracy prior to moving on to the next step in the learning sequence. Frequent checks for understanding (Hattie, 2009; Marzano, 2007; Hunter, 1984) prevent the students from continuing with inaccurate practice or assumptions about the learning.

There are many ways to check for understanding. One of the most popular is for students to indicate with thumbs up—I understand, or thumbs down—I don't understand. Another similar way to indicate personal understanding is to use *fist to five* hand signals: with fist, I do not understand, up to five, I can teach the concept to someone else. While these methods allow students to reflect and offer their perceptions of their progress, these hand signals alone are most likely not an accurate indication of students' progress. Students may give the hand signal that they believe the teacher wants to see. (You can be sure students will not indicate that they are a one.) If hand signals are used, then a follow-up probe of asking a student to share his evidence for why he believes he is a three or four would be important.

More effective checks for understanding include class work on which the teacher checks for understanding in an ongoing method as he circulates around the room during guided and independent practice. As more students use digital resources for their class work, the author has observed checking for understanding to be more difficult as the student's work may not be easily seen while circulating as it was when written on paper. Other effective checks for understanding might sound or look like exit slips, journal notes, reflections, Cornell notes daily summaries, or quick writes. Some examples include:

- Write down a question you believe someone might have about causes of the civil war.
- Write down a sentence of the most important thing you learned today.
- Three things I learned today, two things I'm thinking about, one question I have.
- After reviewing your Cornell notes, write a summary of at least three sentences.

While students are writing, the teacher should be looking at their writing and follow with sharing and clarifications. If exit slips are used, then the responses should serve as evidence to guide the instruction the following day. An example of end-of-class check for understanding was developed by Avis Gainey, social studies teacher at Ocoee Middle School, which shows the expectation of evidence for student's learning, items needing clarification, and the expectation that she will provide feedback (Figure 2.3).

Digital resources may allow for extremely rapid and effective checks for understanding. If students have access to a response system, cell phones, or other devices to respond yes or no, or with a selection from multiple-choice items, within seconds, a teacher can see the variance in accuracy of responses and can follow up with clarifications. If the digital system shows individual names, then the teacher will know who has misunderstandings and can provide correctives individually or differentiate instruction.

FEEDBACK TO IMPROVE LEARNING

When teachers are checking for understanding or reviewing students' work, they provide feedback. There are many forms of feedback, some of which improve the learning outcomes and some that may not do so. To improve learning outcomes feedback should be specific, telling the student what he

Student Self-reflection and Feedback

Monday, month/year

Student Self-reflection and Feedback

Monday, month/year

Today, I learned three new things.

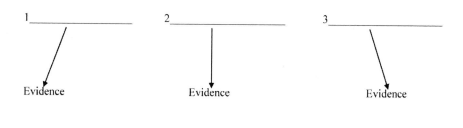

1_____   2_____   3_____

Evidence   Evidence   Evidence

I am still unclear about....

Teacher's Feedback

Figure 2.3.   Check for Understanding. Created by Avis Gainey.

did correctly and why it is correct, and what the student did incorrectly and what would make the response correct (Hattie, 2009; Marzano, 2007). Effective feedback is close to the work, so in designing student work teachers should consider the time it takes to provide quality feedback that will improve learning.

An economics teacher reduced the length of the students' writing assignments with the intent of providing quality feedback. Afterward, he reported to the author that students' work was better and it was actually easier for him to provide feedback on shorter assignments, even though he gave more assignments. More frequent assignments and assessments with quality feedback are effective in improving learning when compared to longer, less frequent assignments with less effective feedback (Roediger, & Karpicke, 2006; Dempster, 1997). Length of the work does not assure rigor or improvement in learning.

Recently, when the authors were in a class for English learners (ELs) the students received their writing assignments back, which were graded on a six-point rubric. On one student's paper was written "2.5, details, transitions." When he showed the author the paper, she gave him specific feedback that the introduction clearly stated his thinking and was a good beginning for the essay. She added that perhaps he had needed more time to generate details to support the introduction. Neither the author nor the student could decipher from the score or the two words what was correct and why nor what was incorrect, except he needed more details and transition words. This is a nonexample of providing feedback to improve learning, or in this case, skill in writing. Other nonexamples are grades, smiley or frowning faces, or other symbols that do not provide explicit assistance in improving learning.

Oral responses to students that generate learning follow the same precepts as those on written work. Respecting the student who offers the response is critical, whether the response is correct or not. Teaching students that you will probe, you will ask for their evidence, or their thinking is helpful as you endeavor to understand how they arrived at particular conclusions or responses. Here are a few examples to think about incorporating whether a response is incorrect or correct.

- Help me understand your thinking.
- Would you share with me the evidence that led you to that response?
- That is an interesting way to look at the situation. How did you arrive at that conclusion?

Also, be sure students have the opportunity to correct misunderstandings. If one student has a misunderstanding, then others will also. The teacher may ask, "How many of you agree or disagree with Gwyn?" Ask those who agree and those who disagree to share their evidence and then ask again how many agree or disagree. Follow up with Gwyn, allowing her and the other students to think through the question and response arriving at the correct one. Notice that the feedback is generative. It generates further thinking by students for them to arrive at the correct understanding. Note that the examples did not have the teacher repeating correct answers nor giving students the answers.

PRACTICAL STEPS FOR LEADERS

- Collaboratively develop non-negotiables for instruction.
- Collaboratively develop and expect implementation of a scaffolded or gradual-release instructional model.
- Provide time for teachers to plan for effective instruction.
- Ask teachers, "Who is successful and how do you know? Under what conditions is each student successful?"

PRACTICAL STEPS FOR TEACHERS

- Plan instruction with other professionals who teach the same discipline, grade, or topic.
- Investigate modules at www.literacydesigncollaborative.org/.
- Gather student success data as you teach so that you know when to move to the next step and with whom to intervene or adjust instruction.
- Teach collaboratively, assess individually.

USEFUL ACADEMIC LANGUAGE

Automaticity—Overlearning to have fluency with a skill or content. Overlearning multiplication tables allows for rapid retrieval of mathematics facts.

Benchmark—Learning target that is a component of a larger standard.

Engage—Motivate students to think and to engage cognitively, not physically.

Generative feedback—Encourages students to think and creates motivation to learn.

Learning target—The intended outcome of the lesson or instruction.

Learning task—The work or task that students engage in to achieve the benchmark or learning target.

Overlearn—Learn to automaticity.

Proficiency—Consistency in demonstrating accuracy with appropriate rate.

Scaffold—Provide high support for success in learning, gradually taking the scaffold or supports away until the students demonstrate proficiency independently.

Chapter Three

Academic Language

Vocabulary has always been important for listening with understanding, for reading with comprehension, and for communication of what has been learned through writing. The Common Core State Standards (CCSS) require comprehension of more general academic language and more discipline-specific vocabulary in earlier grades than previously incorporated in many schools. In middle and high school, the expectation is that students develop fluency with general academic language and discipline-specific language appropriately aligned with moderate to high levels of thinking and complexity. General academic language and discipline-specific academic language are incorporated in CCSS assessments and in the written communication items, which address various disciplines.

GENERAL ACADEMIC LANGUAGE

Instruction in vocabulary and phrases needs to increase to include not only everyday language (Tier 1), but also general academic language (Tier 2). General academic language includes the words and phrases found in textbooks, directions, and learning tasks. Examples include sequence, summarize, solve, explain, and think. Teachers may have the misconception that students have mastery of this language, when in fact, lack of mastery may be part of the reason for lower-than-expected performance on assessments. Please see Chapter 5 relating to English Learners (ELs) and levels of English acquisition.

Common general academic language includes question words (*who, what, when, where,* and *how*). These simple words are learned in kindergarten or first grade and often are posted in the elementary classroom to remind students to identify those elements while reading. As teachers introduce new vocabulary to elementary students, they typically practice pronunciation and add them to other words and names posted under the alphabet, mixing general academic language and common language: A has *and, apple, add, Angela*; B has *ball, begin, Bob,* etc. These tend to be high-frequency words or words that are heard or read over and over again, some of which have little meaning, but have grammatical purpose like articles (*a, the*), prepositions (*to, for*), and conjunctions (*and, or*). Elementary teachers may begin the day with a review of pronunciation of the words or in asking students for meanings of important words.

In intermediate and higher grades, students need facility with more challenging academic language, but use of common academic language may continue: *tell, explain,* and *describe*. For such words, middle- and high-school teachers should substitute general academic language more appropriate to the higher expectations of the grade level: *relate, interpret,* and *specify*. Instead of the elementary words (*who, what, when, where,* and *how*), it would be better to incorporate language such as *character, event, timeframe, location,* and *action*.

Two examples of items students may encounter in texts and assessments follow and illustrate the need of teaching general academic language. "Trace the steps you took to solve the problem" and "Which sentence best illustrates the author's purpose?" *Trace* is employed rather than *sequence* or *tell,* and *illustrate* is employed rather than *describe*. Both represent general academic vocabulary that many students would not comprehend, regardless of grade level, simply because they attribute other meanings to these two words. It would be common for students to believe that *trace* means to draw or outline with a paper over a visual representation, and students may interpret *illustrate* to mean draw a picture, which could lead to incorrect responses. These two examples show sample general academic language that young students need to learn in the early grades and with which they need continued practice and expansion through high school. If students do not comprehend and cannot apply general academic language, then they will not understand directions or perhaps the items on assessments such as CCSS, ACT, and SAT.

Table 3.1 displays sample less rigorous academic language and more rigorous academic language that may be substituted as appropriate to support higher student performance. The language in the right-hand column provides alternatives to expand students' language. It is more rigorous as the words relate to higher levels of thinking and cognitive complexity or are less commonly heard during instruction and yet appear in texts and on assessments. As an example, *compare* is commonly used to identify similarities within one text while *apply* means to think of similarities in another text, the world, or life, extending the thinking beyond the text. *Predict* is most commonly used, when *hypothesize, conjecture,* and *formulate* are examples of more rigorous language. These concepts are shared in detail with examples in Chapter 4.

DISCIPLINE-SPECIFIC LANGUAGE

In specific communication that is oral or written, students demonstrate fluency with everyday language (Tier 1), general academic vocabulary (Tier 2), and discipline-specific academic vocabulary (Tier 3). In English Language Arts (ELA) students encounter words like *fiction, nonfiction, informational text, literary elements*, and *figurative language*, some of which may have been introduced as early as first grade. However, other students may have been limited by minimal introduction of academic language related to ELA prior to middle school. As an example, the authors have observed that many elementary teachers refer to all text as a *story*, when *fiction, nonfiction*, or *informational text* would be the correct categories.

CCSS of Mathematical Practice refer to precise mathematical communication related to definitions, supporting claims, and the problem-solving process. For precision in communication, challenging language has to be learned that includes words like *exponents, multiple, denominator, variable*, and *solution sets*. A common observation of those teaching mathematics without deep knowledge of mathematics is that they appear to avoid use of mathematical academic language. While hesitancy to use mathematical language is observed the most in elementary and middle schools, lack of precision in mathematical communication is not restricted to these levels, reducing the modeling for students and practicing by students with accurate academic mathematical language.

On one such occasion when visiting mathematics classes the division of fractions was being practiced. The teacher was heard saying *flip* rather than

Table 3.1. Less Rigorous and More Rigorous General Academic Language Examples

Less Rigorous Academic Language	More Rigorous General Academic Language
Compare	Connect, Categorize, Apply, Distinguish
Tell, Discuss	Restate, Articulate, Illustrate, Paraphrase
Write	Compose, Formulate, Develop
Explain	Specify, Infer, Analyze, Organize
Right There	Explicit, Identify
Between the Lines	Implicit, Inference, Interpretation
Details	Evidence, Support, Justifications, Reasons
Retell, Recall	Summarize, Show, Generate
Prediction	Hypothesis, Conjecture, Formula

using *reciprocal* or *inverse*. Another teaching geometry used the phrase *around the circle* rather than *circumference*. Rather than using the former language, the teacher should model while using accurate academic language. An advantage of using accurate academic language for ELs is that it is more likely that these terms have cognates in students' home language, particularly if it is Latinate in origin such as Spanish, French, Italian, Romanian, or Portuguese. Accountability for mathematics outcomes has assured that time for instruction is adequate; the issue is deliberate and purposeful incorporation of accurate specific academic language by teachers and students.

Social studies language is less difficult for most students than is the language of mathematics and science. However, it may not be for ELs, since much of mathematics and science language may be similar and the concepts may be demonstrated. With the emphasis on more time for reading and mathematics due to accountability, less time is dedicated to social studies instruction in elementary schools than prior to 2002. Specific social studies language includes terms like *map, geographic features, regions, culture, economy, and timeline*. As a result, students may need more time dedicated to learning the language of social studies, which will pay off with increases in comprehension when reading related texts or passages in assessments. In schools where time for social studies is minimal, it is suggested that during time allocated to reading or ELA that social studies–related passages be incorporated to build specific academic language and use of the resources found in social studies texts: maps, charts, graphs, photographs, and art.

It seems that science has the most difficult specific academic language. This perception may be due to the lack of incorporation of time for science in early grades and lack of deep knowledge of science by elementary teachers. Therefore, the words appear unfamiliar when students first encounter them in upper elementary, middle, or high school. Examples of new-sounding words in life sciences include *arthropod, crustacean, microorganism, protist*, and *ecosystem*. Physical science words may sound familiar, but have specific scientific meanings, like *earth's crust, distance, rate*, and *matter*. Although science texts have many difficult vocabulary words, they tend to be grouped around concepts. When related words are learned together, the difficulty of learning so many groups of new words may be eased. Like social studies language, science vocabulary and concepts should be introduced as early as kindergarten with well-selected science-related texts to be used during time allocated for reading or ELA.

RESEARCH-BASED VOCABULARY INSTRUCTION

One of the easiest methods to assure students' acquisition of any vocabulary, including general and specific academic language, is modeling by the teacher. When teachers are purposeful and deliberate in their use of academic language, students learn it through both direct instruction and through application. As the teacher models accurate academic language and then expects students to use accurate academic language during purposeful talk and other learning tasks, oral fluency develops. An example that comes to mind took place when the author was visiting in a middle school and a mathematics teacher asked, "When will students stop saying *take-away?*" The author's response was, "Students will stop saying *take-away* when you stop accepting the words. When this happens, consider asking students, can you think of mathematical words?"

It may appear harmless to use other words in place of academic language, but these are missed opportunities for language acquisition. Such misconceived practice has the potential to impair students' understanding and perhaps even advancement in discipline-specific learning and performance on assessments. Teachers' expectations for students' language practice should be aligned with those of the texts they read and the assessments they take.

Vocabulary Instruction Protocol

Although there is a plethora of research that supports the lack of effectiveness of long vocabulary lists and the practice of students looking up definitions, these practices continue. There is a growing number of teachers who have adopted research-based vocabulary instructional practices. They begin with students pronouncing the words (yes, even in high school), along with viewing a nonlinguistic representation, the generation of a reasonable definition, and investigating how the word is used in context.

During a visit to a high school EL reading class, the teacher was observed introducing vocabulary prior to the reading. He had developed an interactive presentation that began with the word *sophisticated* on the screen. Then, a photo appeared of James Bond in a tuxedo looking very sophisticated. The students chorally practiced pronunciation, followed by generation of the meaning of sophisticated: smart, nerd, dress cool. After some laughter and discussion, the teacher whisked the visual away revealing a reasonable definition of *sophisticated* and a sentence out of the text to be read that provided meaning in context for *sophisticated* and oral language practice for the ELs.

The same protocol was followed with the next four words. Note that the teacher introduced the words at the time of need and engaged the students' thinking. Also, he limited the words to five, a small enough amount that the students could keep them in short-term memory. In contrast to the compliant behavior usually observed when students are looking up definitions, students were engaged and enjoyed the instruction. The protocol used was

- limiting the number of words introduced to seven or less,

- pronouncing the word,
- providing and developing a reasonable definition,
- providing and developing a nonlinguistic representation, and
- comprehending the word in context (Taylor, 2007; Marzano, Pickering, & Pollock, 2001).

Incorporation of the nonlinguistic representation increases the retention of the word by 30%! This protocol is not enough to move the word to long-term memory as students need to interact with new information over and over again in different ways. If you think about ways to practice vocabulary over and over again, you will easily generate examples similar to these: reading in context, class discussion, purposeful talk, note taking, and writing.

Instructional Strategies

To facilitate the access to skill in deciphering words and practice in deciphering words without directly studying them, teachers can instruct the morphology: roots, prefixes, and suffixes. Knowing these word parts helps students to determine meanings independently. About 55% of regularly used English language comes from Latin. Also, each discipline has specific roots, prefixes, and suffixes that are repeated throughout courses. As an example, social studies has many Latin-based words and science has many German-based words.

With the growing number of students whose primary home language is Spanish, teaching cognates helps students understand English meanings. Examples include *matematica, mapa, francés,* and *planeta.* The same strategy will assist students whose home language is Italian, Portuguese, Romanian, and French since these are Romance languages that developed from Latin. Learning the Latin word parts promotes English academic-language acquisition by these students also.

Using an English and primary home-language dictionary may help some students also, particularly if it is electronic and provides oral language support. One of the issues with a dictionary is that multiple definitions will be provided. Unless the student can determine the correct definition by the use of the word in context, looking up a word may be time consuming and not yield positive outcomes.

Graphic organizers can help students in having deeper understanding of important academic language. They are effective in guided practice when pairs create a graphic organizer with the target words that includes: word, definition in the students' own words, an example, and a nonexample. For learning abstract concepts, nonexamples can be particularly helpful in assisting students in clarifying what the word means. Nonlinguistic representations can be helpful additions to the graphic. The reader will notice that the elements of the graphic organizer include the components in the vocabulary instruction protocol.

Inclusion of synonyms and antonyms in a graphic organizer supports thinking and the development of more precise language. With science and mathematics vocabulary, the teacher may select to use *is* and *is not* in place of synonym and antonym since many of those terms do not have opposites. Graphic organizers can be made into gamelike learning with one of the components provided instead of the target word, and the students have to think to complete the other sections of the graphic organizer.

Interactive word walls represent student engagement and acquisition of vocabulary. The interactive word wall has the components of the vocabulary protocol: word, definition in a student's words, example in context, and a nonlinguistic representation. As students are learning the words, they make cards or graphic organizers and post them on the word wall. When students need vocabulary support they have the interactive word wall as a resource in their classroom. They can also add a synonym or antonym to the word wall. Another interaction may be to group the words by concepts or units as time progresses.

In visiting an elementary school in rural Kentucky the author was impressed that a third-grade teacher had a general word wall, a word wall for science, and one for mathematics. One entire classroom wall was covered in words that the students were to have learned so far that year. *Urban* was one of the words and the author thought it would be wonderful if these students understood the concept. As she had discussions with the students, she pointed to the word and asked students what it meant. Each one pronounced the word as if the pronunciation was the meaning. When students were probed for meaning, they all referred the author to another student or to the teacher.

In this example, the well-meaning teacher posted words she had directly instructed on during reading. On the word wall is where the words remained. Students had limited interaction with the word and there was no resource to remind students of the meaning of words like *urban* with which they had no personal experience. Therefore, they did not acquire the new vocabulary word *urban*. Word walls are intended to support learning, not to be words on a wall that teachers post.

Digital resources that allow students to play with the language in engaging ways, like the jeopardy example provided in Chapter 2, are also beneficial. In addition to playing with language, there are digital resources that adjust to individual students' progress and pronounce words for students, check their vocabulary progress, and provide immediate feedback to the students and data to the teacher. Students who have digital resources may develop and retain their personally developed resources with the components of research-based vocabulary acquisition on their devices.

EXPECTED LANGUAGE-ACQUISITION OUTCOMES

Academic language acquisition is not optional if students are to be successful on CCSS-related assessments, and if improvement on college admissions assessments is a goal. Teachers, who are experts in their disciplines, may resist the expectation of directly teaching, modeling, and practicing general academic language and discipline-specific language.

A mathematics teacher was compliant in implementing the academic vocabulary instructional expectations, although he said to the author, "I resent having to do this." After success with the vocabulary instruction protocol, he found that time was saved during problem solving and that he had a smoother flow to instruction. Mathematical reasoning was not interrupted for him to explain the language used. Once teachers implement research-based vocabulary instruction at the point of need, they find that the instructional process goes more smoothly and students become more proficient with the learning target.

PRACTICAL STEPS FOR LEADERS

- Employ teachers and staff who model correct English and academic language orally and in writing, in all grades and disciplines.
- During walkthroughs and class visits, look for student-developed resources rather than professionally or teacher-made resources.
- Encourage student-made interactive word walls.
- Listen for students and faculty using academic language.
- Model academic language for faculty and students.
- Reinforce teachers' modeling of correct and formal English in speaking and writing.

PRACTICAL STEPS FOR TEACHERS

- Use nonlinguistic representations to create mental models of vocabulary.
- Ask students to paraphrase definitions and others' words.
- Use digital resources that provide fluent pronunciations.
- Teach, model, and practice academic language that is general or specific to the discipline.
- Use dictionaries as resources, not as text from which definitions are to be copied.
- Teach roots, prefixes, and suffixes specific to the discipline.
- Use cognates to link primary home language to English.

USEFUL ACADEMIC LANGUAGE

Fluent—Appropriate rate and accuracy.

Interactive word walls—Words, definitions, examples, visuals that students use as they progress with a learning task.

Nonlinguistic representation—Without words.

Purposeful talk—Specific short discussions using academic language that take place during guided practice.

Chapter Four

Rigor—Levels of Thinking, Cognitive Complexity, and Text Complexity

With the introduction of the Common Core State Standards (CCSS), attention has turned to rigor in planning instruction for students' success on the aligned assessments. The authors define rigor as *expectations for students' learning related to levels of thinking, cognitive complexity, and/or text complexity of the learning resources aligned with CCSS.* These expectations of rigor would be considered proficient (on grade level on accountability assessments) on CCSS. This chapter will deepen understanding of rigor, in terms of thinking, cognitive complexity, and text complexity specifically through application to CCSS.

MAKING SENSE OF LEVELS OF THINKING
AND COGNITIVE COMPLEXITY

Understanding CCSS expectations requires building on what readers know about levels of thinking, which they most probably associate with undergraduate courses that included the taxonomy of educational objectives (Bloom et al., 1956). In building on readers' knowledge related to levels of thinking the addition of Webb's depth of knowledge (Webb, 2005) is helpful. This section will illustrate both levels of thinking and depth of knowledge to arrive at clarity for addressing text complexity as referenced in CCSS.

Levels of Thinking

Bloom and others have endeavored to categorize levels of thinking from that which is factual or low level and thinking that requires the creation of new knowledge. At the lowest level of recall or knowledge teachers ask questions like where, who, what, and when. Such information is explicitly stated in a text. The second level of thinking is comprehension or understanding and is common in classrooms and in texts: compare, contrast, retell, sequence, discuss, and paraphrase. Like the lowest level of knowledge, comprehension is also in the text, but the reader has to read more to pull together information from more than one place in the text. These two levels of thinking are those most commonly heard and seen in classrooms, but not favored in CCSS.

The third level of thinking is application. It requires students to comprehend the text and do something with the information like connect or relate it to previous learning, to demonstrate understanding through performance, or use of the knowledge in some way. This level of thinking takes two steps: comprehend and do something with the knowledge. Therefore, answers to such items are not in the text. Application is the level at which expectations for CCSS begin.

Analysis is the fourth level of thinking and requires the student to take apart what is being learned into its components and then put the information back together. As an example, students might be asked to categorize living and nonliving things, or classify living things as plants or animals. Analysis might also require students to infer, to prioritize, or to diagram. In reading literary texts, the teacher may ask, "What do you infer from the author's tone?" Students must understand the abstract concept of tone and then extrapolate how the tone might relate to the text.

Evaluation is a very high level of thinking and requires students to take several steps. Students have to comprehend, analyze, and apply criteria to the text to make a judgment. Without criteria upon which to make the evaluation, the learning task is at the analysis level of thinking. An algebra-class evaluation scenario might be that students have learned several strategies for solving a problem and are asked to select from the various strategies the one that they prefer based on the criteria of accuracy, applicability, and efficiency. Another evaluation example would be that students are studying the use of figurative language in poetry and are asked to select the poem in which the figurative language is most effective based on the criteria of creating interest and a rich description that evokes a visual image. Academic language such as *assess, discriminate, judge, reframe, justify,* and *defend* is often associated with evaluation. As a level of thinking, evaluation must have criteria upon which the evaluation is based, whether the student develops the criteria or it is part of the instructional content. Teachers should expect students to develop the evaluation based on the criteria and support the evaluation with textual evidence. It is important to note that while evaluation could be expected with one text, higher-level cognitive complexity would be to evaluate across two or more texts as in these examples. Application, analysis, and evaluation are the levels of thinking that form the heart of CCSS expectations.

Cognitive Complexity: Depth of Knowledge (DOK)

Norman Webb developed Depth of Knowledge (DOK) as a way to conceptualize thinking and learning as cognitive complexity. Depth of Knowledge goes beyond the thinking levels provided by Bloom to doing, although the same language is used. In DOK, there are four levels of cognitive complexity or levels of knowing and doing:

- level one—recall,
- level two—skill/concept,
- level three—strategic thinking, and
- level four—extended thinking.

It is important to understand that neither cognitive complexity nor levels of thinking require texts and could apply to various types of learning experiences.

Level one (recall) is similar to the knowledge/recall level of thinking. Level two (skill or concept) is similar to comprehension and application of knowledge, but requires the student to take two or more steps to arrive at the response. The third level of strategic thinking requires the student to take multiple steps and there are multiple correct responses, such as comprehend and then infer, conclude, develop, or apply the content to a new context. Extended thinking is similar to analysis and evaluation, as the student has to investigate and process beyond one text or experience to synthesize and/or bring together various sources to create or design a new product as the evidence of student learning.

The CCSS assessments use a combination of the two ways described for conceptualizing thinking. By designing the Cognitive Rigor Matrix that has Bloom's levels of thinking on the vertical axis and DOK on the horizontal access, a tool has been created that is useful in designing instruction and assessment aligned with CCSS (Hess, Carlock, Jones, & Walkup, 2009). On the National Center for the Improvement of Educational Assessment website (http://nciea.org) readers can find several cognitive rigor matrices: reading, writing, and mathematics/science. These matrices are useful tools for finding academic language and for determining appropriate evidences of students' learning that are aligned with CCSS.

TEXT COMPLEXITY

Text complexity was not created for CCSS, but has certainly been brought to the forefront as a result of the implementation. The CCSS have a separate standard for text complexity making it the center of many educators' conversations (Hiebert & Mesmer, 2013). Text complexity is described in detail in

CCSS ELA Appendix A (NGA Center & CCSSO, 2010) and is summarized here. In contrast to past measures of readability, text complexity is the combination of three types of measures: qualitative text characteristics, quantitative text characteristics, and the interaction of text and the student's preparedness for the learning task (level of thinking or cognitive complexity required) (NGA Center & CCSSO, 2010). Much of the thinking elements are grounded in the work of Bloom and Webb as described in the previous section, but the remainder emerged from the reality of varying elements in text that make it more or less accessible to students and their deep understanding.

Qualitative characteristics of text complexity include the structure related to genres, levels of meaning (figurative or literal), language familiarity, and knowledge required for comprehension. Familiarity of the vocabulary is a contributor whether it is antiquated (ice box/refrigerator), non-English (du jour/of the day), or difficult academic language. Some questions to think about include:

- Is the structure easy to follow or unusual?
- Are there multiple levels of meaning?
- Is the language conventional or is the reader required to slow down and reread for comprehension, looking up unknown words that may be embedded?
- Do students need to have specific knowledge to comprehend the text?

An example of text that would be complex for most 11th-grade students would be *Hamlet*. There are multiple levels of meaning for many phrases. *Hamlet* uses language uncommon to most 11th-grade students, along with figurative language, historical references, as well as other literary references. Students would need background knowledge related to Shakespeare, England and its relationship to Denmark during the period, and how people lived.

Quantitative characteristics are those that can be measured. In this text Lexile Framework is used. It is widely accepted and is an easy tool for teachers to use to identify Lexile associations for texts and to assist in guiding students to ranges. Lexile ranges are quantitatively measured ranges of reading comprehension. Expectations have been adjusted to reflect higher expectations of the CCSS for College and Career Readiness as noted in Chapter 1. Frequency of words, length of sentences, and length of text contribute to the complexity.

The third measure of text complexity is the text and students' learning task interaction. Informational text usually has a clear purpose, challenging vocabulary, and learning tasks at the moderate to high complexity levels, requiring a number of steps to be taken (levels of thinking and cognitive complexity). Literary text complexity is often associated with the meaning of the text, such as literal (low complexity) or figurative and interpretive (high complexity). However, the complexity is specific to any text and the learner's preparedness to succeed with the task.

Depending upon the knowledge that the student is expected to bring to the text and the learning task, the text complexity will vary. Therefore, text complexity does not refer to the text alone, but also refers to the student's preparation to be successful with the learning task.

- To what extent does the reader need to understand history to respond to literary items?
- To what extent does the reader need to know mythology to comprehend the poem?
- In science, does the student need to have a working knowledge of algebra?
- Can students read the text independently and complete the learning tasks or do they need more support as nonproficient readers, under-resourced students, or English Learners (ELs) may?

The more knowledge and comprehension skill students are expected to bring to the text and the learning task presented, the greater the text complexity. As you can see, if teachers are expected to increase the text complexity incorporated into their instruction, it will be essential to consider the background knowledge needed, differentiated instruction, and resources to scaffold learners to success with the learning task at hand.

Misconceptions

Modifying text complexity is a strategy well-meaning teachers may use to provide nonproficient readers with accessible text. The authors have observed instances when this well-meaning effort was detrimental to students' learning. With digital resources, text complexity level can be adjusted downward, making the readability of the text no longer an issue for nonproficient readers. The logic behind this strategy is that if the students can access the text, then they can answer the rigorous questions that follow. On the surface, this seems like a useful practice for differentiating the text without changing the content or expectations of rigorous thinking.

In one particular instance, an elementary fifth-grade teacher modified the Lexile level of an article to allow for all students to be able to comprehend the passage and respond to items in a homework assignment. The next day, when reviewing the homework, the teacher came across a note from a parent stating that the answer to Question 3 was not in the passage. Initially, the teacher marked the question wrong and moved on, but after reflection returned to read the passage and to investigate the parent's comment. After reading the modified passage himself, the teacher realized that the parent was correct; the answer to Question 3 was not in the modified passage. He read a higher Lexile version of the same passage that he had given to more advanced readers and easily found the answer. As the Lexile level was lowered for readability, the text that allowed students to answer the rigorous items was removed.

Similarly, the authors observed a misconception example during collaborative planning with American History teachers. The American History teacher team was examining their texts to pull out key points to use in developing the concept of *imperialism*. When reviewing the advanced version and the on-grade-level version of the textbook, the teachers noted that there were key points contained in the advanced version that were not in the on-grade-level text. Are key points only important for advanced students? The team was disturbed to realize that only the teacher of the advanced students would have taught these important points, while others' students would have missed them if their teachers relied on the designated textbook, although the key points are on the end of course exam required of all students. (To learn more about collaborative planning, please see Chapter 8.) The same analysis of appropriate content and complexity should be applied to digital resources as well.

Effective Use of Text Complexity

In working with teachers at multiple grades authors have identified several tasks that are particularly helpful for teachers to be effective in using text complexity as a concept to improve rigor in instruction. First and most importantly, teachers must closely examine and read text before asking students to do so, determining the appropriateness for their students and any needed instructional differentiation. Second, they must complete the learning tasks that students will be asked to do to be sure they are reasonable and that accurate information is within the text to be read. By doing these two tasks the teacher will be prepared to provide additional support or academic challenges for students who need differentiation to maximize their learning.

CLOSE READING

A strategy to assist teachers in facilitating comprehension of complex text is close reading. It is not a new strategy, but one that successful readers have used and generally includes:

1. reading a quality text selection,
2. rereading as many as three times,
3. annotating the text for specific elements,
4. discussing, and

5. summarizing the purposeful elements being sought in the text (Fang & Pace, 2013).

Various authors propose different steps to this general strategy. One popular sequence is to ask students to read independently, first annotating for specific comprehension elements, such as main idea or literary elements (characters, setting, and plot). The students' independent reading would be followed by partner discussion. Then the teacher would read aloud to the students, followed by class discussion. Keep in mind that to read independently and without assistance as this strategy requires, students must know about 95% of the words. Before using this close reading strategy the teacher should first evaluate if the students can read the text independently.

For students who do not read independently on the level of the text, the authors suggest that the teacher read aloud with students following along first, giving access to those who read two or more grade levels below the text. Then, the students can partner read or read independently (depending on their independent reading level), annotating as directed. Partner discussions, class discussions, and inquiry would follow, concluding with appropriate writing.

In authors' discussions with teachers who have been directed to follow one particular approach to close reading, it has been clear that one approach only is not sufficient. The best approach is the one that considers the students' readiness to read the identified quality text independently, the text complexity, and the cognitive complexity of the learning task. The most important thing to know about close reading is that it does include annotation of text, analysis of text, and thinking by the students.

MOTIVATING STUDENTS

Motivation of students to engage with rigorous learning tasks may be a concern. Motivation is a natural state, but sometimes the conditions in classrooms temporarily demotivate students (Jensen, 1998). Conditions that demotivate students are related to the student's perception of his academic safety, belief in his ability to successfully achieve, or perceived value of the learning task.

Academic safety to learn means that each particular classroom is free of put downs and negative conditions that prevent him from giving 100% to the learning task. It also reflects the resources, physical environment, and the emotional environment.

The student's belief in her ability to be successful on the learning task relates to other chapters in this book on the teachers' responsibility to design scaffolded and differentiated instruction, provide appropriate feedback, and develop a supportive positive relationship with students. The Benchmark Scale with Evidence that is discussed in Chapter 7 is one of the tools shared that can be helpful in assisting students to believe in their success and to monitor their own progress.

The perceived value of the learning task relates to cognitive engagement, which is essential to maximize learning. Teachers may have the misconception that if they entertain students they will enjoy learning or if they do not push them academically they will be happy and learn more. There is no relationship of entertaining students and making them happy with increased learning outcomes. These are misconceptions; student motivation is naturally within and is evident when the learning task is perceived to be doable, worth doing, and respects their ability to think and learn in an academically safe classroom.

Visualize the difference between a classroom in which the teacher simply assigns work and students independently and passively try to complete learning tasks, such as worksheets with low-level thinking items. Consider the lack of motivation and the teacher's possible misconceptions about why students do not appear to put forth effort and/or complete the work.

Now, mentally step down the hall to a science class in which they are engaged in reading a nonfiction text aligned with the Next Generation Science Standards (NGSS) strand of the nature of science, *The Immortal Life of Henrietta Lacks* (Skloot, 2010). Visualize how the teacher presents thought-provoking queries, such as "Is it ethical for a researcher to take your cells without your knowledge, even if the purpose is the help others?" Students take two minutes to discuss this deep question and support it with evidence in their responses. After the class lists the responses, groups the responses into categories, and labels the categories (list-group-label strategy), the science teacher reads compelling sentences to the students while thinking aloud to assure their comprehension.

"Just as there is no law requiring informed consent for storing tissue,
(Think aloud: *Does informed consent mean you have been told what may take place prior to agreeing?*)
there is no clear requirement for telling donors when their tissues might result in profit." (Skloot, 2010, p. 426)
(Think aloud: *Can companies make money from a person's cells?*)

In triads, students eagerly apply what they read to their own lives and other things they have heard of, such as the use of prisoners during World War II for experiments. Not only are students eager to read more about Henrietta Lacks, the donor for the *HeLa* cells that have contributed to the health of many, but also want to learn more about the nature of science and other ethical issues. Working collaboratively in groups to solve real, not hypothetical problems and apply knowledge to real tasks, issues, and situations motivates students. Students are discussing and reflecting on learning. In this visualized classroom, students are more motivated to engage with and complete the task of reading a nonfiction text that aligns with the standards to be learned; it is doable, perceived to be worth doing, and respects them with thinking in an academically safe classroom. Teachers who embrace this type of classroom experience greater success not only in engagement, but in academic achievement as well.

The challenge is to connect the standards-based learning target to something of value to the students—such as their families, lives, heritage, experience, future, and other things they know. By using the strategy of *connection*, students have an entry point and therefore believe they can learn this next segment of curriculum. As an example, when observing a first year teacher introducing students to Reconstruction, the US historical period after the Civil War, the teacher began by showing authentic documents, including political cartoons and hand bills that were posted around towns during the time. As a whole class they analyzed their inferences drawn from these authentic documents and responded to a few items. The students transitioned to guided practice to continue digging more deeply into this period of history in collaborative groups and the class came to closure by drawing conclusions from their review, inferences, readings, and discussions. Examples of the queries provided by this novice teacher follow that accompanied a digital representation of a Reconstruction period hand bills on the Freedman's Bureau.

1. What was the Freedmen's Bureau?
2. Provide two examples with which the Freedmen's Bureau was tasked.
3. How did the Freedmen's Bureau protect African Americans from persecution?
4. Apply the idea of the Freedmen's Bureau to your own life. Have you ever needed assistance in order to better yourself?

As you review these items, underline the academic language within each. Where in the items do the students connect the reconstruction period or the Freedmen's Bureau to their lives? Identify the moderate- to high-level thinking and complexity items, if there are any.

In observing this class, the authors noted that the students were engaged with the learning task. Students believed they would be successful as the teacher scaffolded instruction for historical content that was unknown, but could be connected to their lives. Instead of lecturing to the students on this important period in US history, he respected their ability to think, analyze, infer, and draw conclusions. Effective teachers expect students to think more and tell them less than ineffective teachers do. The rigor and thinking of the learning task added to the motivation of the students, as it communicated the teacher's belief in their ability to be successful. These students enjoyed the learning task because they were successful and the task represented respect for them in an academically safe environment. There was no entertainment by the teacher, but serious and well-planned instruction appropriate for these students.

STUDENT ACADEMIC GOALS

In addition to Benchmark Scales with Evidence (Chapter 7), which students use to monitor their progress on specific learning tasks identified by the teacher, students are also motivated by setting their own academic goals. In some schools, elementary through high school, each student maintains her own data and goal notebook, either print or digital. Within this notebook students have their own data and their own academic goals. They self-monitor and note changes whether improvements or setbacks. With the assistance of respected educators, students can take control of their goals and improvement.

As students are monitoring their progress toward their own academic goals, they should be encouraged to be metacognitive about how they learn best. Teachers and administrators can assist students in being metacognitive by providing them questions similar to those that follow.

• Under what conditions do you do your best work?
• When teachers ask you to use particular learning strategies, which ones seem most effective to you?
• What do you do when you have difficulty understanding a text?

Teachers will be more effective and have more highly motivated students if they engage with the students in setting and monitoring their learning goals. Provide students opportunities to reflect on how they learn best, and then teachers may determine which strategies are most effective from both the students' and teacher's point of view.

WRITING IS THINKING

One of the easiest and most accessible ways to raise the level of thinking is to ask students to write. Writing can be bullets, points to remember, key words, phrases, sentences, paragraphs, and longer pieces. Writing to foster thinking does not have to be a five-paragraph essay. It needs to be academically safe, beginning with success and then building to longer pieces and more complex writing. Writing is a higher cognitive process than reading or speaking and is a natural way to check for understanding and for students to show their thinking.

Many disciplines use quick writes, sentence starters, or *what if?* to stimulate thinking. In mathematics, The Standards for Mathematical Practice include communicating mathematically (orally and in writing) because of the thinking required to do so. Teachers can provide mathematics students with several strategies to solve a problem and let them choose the one each prefers. Then, students should justify why they chose a particular strategy, apply it followed by a written explanation of why it did or did not work as expected, aligned with *Standard 3 Construct viable arguments and critique reasoning of others.*

Disciplines lend themselves to various forms of writing that are appropriate for the developmental stage and writing proficiency of students. In science students can develop their written communication while using academic language and content standards through reasoned argument. Reasoned argument includes a question, assumptions, claim(s), evidence, explanation, and rebuttal (Llewellyn, 2013). By students collaboratively addressing an issue or problem with these steps, they have support, but also must think at high levels because they have to present both sides of the posed question. Reasoned argument is an excellent strategy for helping students to separate pseudoscience and science fiction from empirically supported science. The same strategy can be used in other disciplines as well.

PRACTICAL STEPS FOR LEADERS

- Provide time and space for teachers to preview and analyze text prior to instruction.
- Prepare facilitators (teacher leaders, instructional coaches, administrators) to assist teachers during common planning until independence as fully functioning collaborative teams is achieved.
- Monitor the enhancement of students' levels of thinking, cognitive complexity, and text complexity of resources used in instruction.
- Provide opportunities for teachers across disciplines to compare standards and levels of thinking to draw conclusions of how the rigor is aligned.
- Provide teachers with professional learning to consider strategies to assist students with deep comprehension of quality text.
- Fund the purchase of quality nonfiction texts to use for engagement and teaching of standards.

PRACTICAL STEPS FOR TEACHERS

- Include at least one learning task that requires moderate to high levels of thinking and cognitive complexity each day.
- Have students reflect weekly on which learning tasks helped them learn the most.
- Reflect on the level of thinking and cognitive complexity expected across a unit of study and how to appropriately enhance the rigor.
- Infuse quality texts aligned with standards that relate to students' lives and the things they value.
- Incorporate close reading strategies appropriate for your students, text, and discipline.

USEFUL ACADEMIC LANGUAGE

Authentic documents—Hand bills, cartoons, visuals, pictures, and so on that are not created for instruction, but are copies of original ones. These artifacts assist students in engaging with the time and place as they respond to document based questions.

Cognitive complexity—Developed by Norman Webb it is often referred to as Depth of Knowledge (DOK). It relates to the steps needed to complete a learning task or to respond to an item and is rated from low to high complexity.

Levels of thinking—Based on the work of Bloom et al. (1956) the levels range from factual or information stated in one place in a text, to application, evaluation, and creation of new knowledge.

Text complexity—Describes the student's challenge in interacting successfully with the text. It is the interaction of multiple dynamics including the student's background knowledge and skill needed, the Lexile and other quantitative measures, and qualitative measures such as the conventional or unconventional language, and levels of meanings.

Reasoned argument—Structured process used in science and other disciplines to provide access to thinking and organizing thinking in a meaningful way that can be communicated to others.

Chapter Five

English Learners and CCSS

Do educators need to consider English learners (ELs) separately from other Pk–12 students when addressing academic rigor, student engagement, and high achievement? Are ELs' needs different from other students' needs in meeting the more challenging Common Core State Standards (CCSS)? Both of these questions can be answered with *yes* and *no*. Like many other complex issues in education, the needs of ELs depend on multiple factors. Fortunately, a substantial number of factors that affect ELs also affect their peers who are native speakers of English. These commonalities are a strong basis from which to provide effective leading and teaching strategies for EL students' learning. However, what defines ELs—their still-developing proficiency in listening, speaking, reading, and writing English as a second language—sets their needs apart from other students, requiring the same strategies known to be effective for others, plus *something more*.

The premise of this book, that all students can meet rigorous expectations if given appropriate support, certainly encompasses ELs. Melissa Hancock, Oak Ridge High School literacy coach and effective reading teacher communicated her belief this way.

> We have to set our expectations high. If we don't, how else can they get where they need to be? They are capable of doing the same work as non-ESOL students; they just need extra support and scaffolding to get there.

Educators of ELs must hold true to this goal of access to excellence and equity. Providing scaffolding, academic language development, and higher-order thinking practice is crucial for ELs to reach the highest standards of achievement, just as it is for all students. Likewise, giving specific feedback and communicating learning goals through Benchmark Scales with Evidence, can be powerful motivators for ELs' learning, engaging them in the process of acquiring all aspects of English proficiency and in achieving grade-level expectations in academic subject learning.

This chapter addresses teaching ELs in the discipline-specific classroom, such as language arts, science, social studies, and mathematics. This is in contrast to the English class for speakers of other languages that is intensely focused on English-language acquisition, instead of the discipline-specific focus. Unless otherwise noted, when *native speaker* is used in this chapter, the intention is the native English-speaking student who achieves at proficient in English on the accountability assessment, although many native speakers are not at the proficient level.

SOMETHING MORE

So what does the *something more* that distinguishes ELs' needs from other students look and sound like? This difference relates primarily to language's impact on curriculum, instruction, and assessment. Because ELs are not yet fully proficient in listening and speaking (oral language) as well as reading and writing (print language) in English, they need additional types of support depending on their current level of English proficiency. They also may need more time to reach the same English Language Arts (ELA) standards as native-speaking peers. This does not mean more time as in longer test administrations, although that may be an appropriate accommodation for some students. Instead, more time means that ELs with no English communication, who enter schools where English is the language of instruction, will likely take more than the school year to reach grade-level proficiency in English listening, speaking, reading, and writing, especially for academic-language use. Bilingual education researcher Jim Cummins (1984) found that depending on age of arrival to an English-speaking school, ELs can take five to seven years to develop proficient or the grade-level expectation academic-language use in English oral language and literacy. Other researchers, such as Virginia Collier and Wayne Thomas (2004), found it can take from 7 to 10 years to develop English proficiency. However, the reality is that these students are accountable for demonstrating learning gains on accountability assessments like native speakers, even if not yet proficient in English.

The time it takes to learn another language, or to reach proficiency, and to achieve academic ELA standards, is affected by many factors. The age at which the learner begins to acquire a second language has a major impact on time to proficiency. A child who entered school in kindergarten and was just beginning to listen, speak, read, and write in English will have a decidedly different experience from a ninth-grader with similar English skills. Age is not the only factor, however. Another factor in English acquisition relates to the influence of the home; ELs whose parents have higher levels of education and are English proficient most probably will acquire English proficiency more quickly than others.

Individual aptitude for learning second languages can affect the proficiency timeline as well. Some learners have great facility with language, a linguistic intelligence or ability to identify and analyze a language's parts and assemble them correctly. These are helpful skills when learning a new language.

Because this book focuses on how leading and teaching affect learning, it emphasizes the second-language acquisition factors that administrators, teacher leaders, instructional coaches, and classroom teachers have the greatest influence over, the *something more* that ELs need, not factors that educators cannot impact (for example, the student's age or aptitude). The discussion of the *something more* that ELs need begins with a description of the common features of ELs' English proficiency in four major groupings (Levels 1–6 refer to the World-Class Instructional Design and Assessment (WIDA) English language development (ELD) Standards, discussed in the WIDA Language Proficiency Levels section):

a. Levels 1 & 2, what we term Beginning ELs;
b. Levels 3 & 4, what we term Intermediate ELs;
c. Level 5, what we term Advanced ELs; and
d. Level 6, what we term Exited/Monitored ELs.

Understanding how these levels of proficiency affect students' ability to meet CCSS standards is a solid foundation for providing appropriate support and setting rigorous, yet realistic expectations. By holding to rigorous yet realistic expectations of achievement of ELs in English given their current level of proficiency, and by providing the appropriate support for meeting these expectations, educators can accelerate the process of second-language acquisition and elevate ELs' ultimate levels of oral language and literacy attainment in English (Ellis, 2008).

LEVELS OF ENGLISH PROFICIENCY

Chances are at some point in school you studied a foreign language, say Spanish, French, or maybe even German. Many adults report that after studying a language for two years or more, they can't even hold a basic conversation. What a pity. That is why there is a booming industry for foreign language programs, be they computer-based, online, or immersion abroad. If learning a second language were easy and quick, these companies would have to sell something else to adults who did not learn the other subjects well enough in high school (or college). If you have tried to learn another language, either through formal study or by moving somewhere it is spoken, you probably need no further convincing that it takes time, effort, guidance, explanation, practice, and motivation to succeed in your goal. And you probably realize that if you were transferred to a small town in Uzbekistan, for instance, it would take you a while to pick up the Uzbek language. And it would be mostly Uzbek for basic survival purposes at that. Once you learned how to order recognizable food in a restaurant, would you then feel ready to write a five-paragraph essay in grammatically perfect Uzbek on the conquest of Transoxiana (the territory between the Amudarya and Syrdarya Rivers), after having listened to an hour-long lecture delivered in Uzbek on the history of the region? It sounds pretty impossible, does it not?

This chapter could argue that holding you to the standard "Write informative/explanatory texts, including the narration of historical events" . . . using "varied transitions and sentence structures to link the major sections of the text, . . . precise language, and . . . convey a knowledgeable stance in a style that responds to the discipline context" (CCSS Grades 11–12 Writing Standard for Literacy in History/Social Studies, Science, and Technical Subjects) in Uzbek would certainly be rigorous, but it would not be realistic given your beginning level of Uzbek proficiency. The same would be true for an 11th-grade beginning EL in a US History class using the CCSS Writing Standards—rigorous but unrealistic.

But, of course, not all ELs are beginners, and as they progress to higher levels of English proficiency, the distance between an academic subject's language demands and the student's English proficiency is expected to diminish. The challenge for all teachers of ELs is to provide appropriate support for rigorous academic subject learning and second-language development, while holding in mind what is realistic for an EL at a particular level of English proficiency. Learning academic content in a second language is cognitively complex and is cognitively demanding on the learner. To assist the reader in gaining a better sense of the contrast between grade-level ELA CCSS expectations and characteristics of specific levels of EL English proficiency, the next section describes each of the proficiency groupings in light of sample grade-level standards and their adaptations for ELs.

WIDA LANGUAGE PROFICIENCY LEVELS

Developed by the WIDA organization, a consortium including 33 states, the WIDA language proficiency levels divide the progression from beginning to exited English learner into six levels. It is helpful for any educator to become familiar with each of the six levels' descriptors (please see http://wida.us to review the complete document), but using the details of all six of them to provide the *something more* that ELs need (differentiation for ELs) can be somewhat overwhelming for a classroom teacher of ELs mixed among a majority of native speakers. For practical purposes, this chapter has clustered the six WIDA levels into three levels of differentiation: Beginning, Intermediate, and Advanced English Learner. The sixth level WIDA identifies, *Reaching*, is intended for ELs who have met grade-level English proficiency and require the same type of instructional support that native speakers need as described in other chapters. For this reason, this chapter does not specify this proficiency level for purposes of instructional differentiation. Table 5.1 describes each of the three levels of differentiation for which the authors advocate in every classroom with ELs.

Looking at the major level categories, one can see a progression that builds from understanding and using single, frequent words and common, simple phrases to being able to express oneself completely in novel, complex, and connected sentences using social as well as academic language for general and discipline-specific purposes. While it is certainly possible to express complex concepts and relationships without language, such as with visual diagrams, no one can deny the important role of language in conveying this type of complicated information and it is how students' proficiency is measured on CCSS assessments, the ACT, the SAT, and on other respected assessments. The increasing emphasis on academic-language development for all students underscores the crucial function of language in academic-subject learning, and when academic disciplines are taught primarily through language, there is an interaction between the concepts being learned and the language used to teach and learn them. This is particularly challeng-

Table 5.1. English Proficiency Levels

Differentiation Level	WIDA Level	Learner Language Complexity and Forms
Beginning	1 2	Everyday single words, simple, formulaic phrases for common situations and objects, repetitive phrase and sentence patterns
Intermediate	3 4	Short sentences with growing complexity, repetitive grammatical structures with some variety in sentence patterns, specific discipline vocabulary and expressions, use of idioms and polysemous words
Advanced	5	Complex sentences, cohesive and coherent expression, appropriate grammatical structures for purpose, variety of sentence patterns, technical and abstract disciplinary language, various connotations of words and expressions
Exited	6	Exited English learners have the same proficiency as native speakers, but they require continuous monitoring for slippage or lack of progress.

ing for ELs, whose English (the language of teaching and learning in mainstream classrooms) is developing at the same time their mastery of the new disciplinary topics, academic language, and concepts is developing. Because of this complex interaction ELs have a bigger job in learning academic subjects than native speakers, and ELs at the beginning level have the most arduous job of all. For these students, educators must provide a greater degree of support and must be realistic in their expectations for how and when they can meet grade-level expectations.

Beginning English Learners

It is helpful to look at an example for a beginning EL in seventh grade. The CCSS lists *Narrative of the Life of Frederick Douglass an American Slave, Written by Himself* as a grades 6–8 appropriate informational text read in language arts or social studies. Scaffolding of the historical context and the historical figure, Frederick Douglas, with visuals or digital resources would build background knowledge that would prepare all students for understanding this informational text. The following is the first six sentences of the first paragraph:

> The plan which I adopted, and the one by which I was most successful, was that of making friends of all the little white boys whom I met in the street. As many of these as I could, I converted into teachers. With their kindly aid, obtained at different times and in different places, I finally succeeded in learning to read. When I was sent of errands, I always took my book with me, and by going one part of my errand quickly, I found time to get a lesson before my return. I used also to carry bread with me, enough of which was always in the house, and to which I was always welcome; for I was much better off in this regard than many of the poor white children in our neighborhood. This bread I used to bestow upon the hungry little urchins, who, in return, would give me that more valuable bread of knowledge.

The CCSS Reading Standards for Informational Text Grade 7 specify that the student should cite textual evidence to analyze explicit and inferential points made, determine the meaning of figurative, connotative, and technical words and phrases used, and assess the evidence used to make the claims. For a beginning EL, who understands and uses single words and simple, formulaic phrases and sentence patterns, being able to extract meaning from the seventh-grade text in English would require a herculean amount of scaffolding, which would involve some amount of translation into the native language to comprehend. In fact, the structure of the very first sentence involves relative clauses, which are more typical of high intermediate- to advanced-level English learners. There is a lot going on between the subject (plan) and verb (was) of the first sentence, and it takes a higher level of English proficiency to be able to even pull the sentence elements apart.

> The plan
> *which* I adopted, [I adopted the plan]
> and the *one* [the plan]
> by *which* I was most successful, [I used the plan most successfully]
> was
> *that of* making friends [I became friends]
> of all the little white boys [with all the little white boys]
> *whom* I met in the street. [I met the boys in the street].

For a beginning EL, an entire class period could be devoted to breaking down the structure and meaning of this very first sentence. The reference words *which* and *whom* not only need to be connected to their antecedents (the words to which they refer), but their placement within the sentence and the words surrounding them need to be explained and defined. The details of the analysis described are important since their structure is beyond a beginning EL's acquired grammatical competence in English. Certainly, this is an unusually worded sentence, but most native speakers would be able to restate the general meaning of the sentence in simpler terms (He had a successful plan. He became friends with all the little white boys he met on the street.), something a beginning EL could not yet do.

An advanced EL, who understands and uses a variety of complex sentences, structures for cohesion and purpose, and connotations of technical and abstract language, would not need the same degree of unpacking and should be able to restate the sentence. In the case of the advanced EL, a quick pointing out of the relative pronouns, *which, that,* and *whom* and their antecedents could help check for accurate comprehension. On the other hand, an analysis and unpacking of each sentence to the degree modeled here for the beginning ELs would not be necessary, not to mention that moving at this pace would not allow for completion of many texts!

So, to enable a seventh-grade beginning EL to *cite textual evidence to analyze explicit and inferential points made, determine the meaning of figurative, connotative, and technical words and phrases used, and assess the evidence used to make the claims,* the teacher would need to provide a text whose grammatical structures are simple, common, and frequent (in other words, at the level of the EL's proficiency) or she would need to meticulously unpack, and use translation to help comprehension of a seventh-grade text. What is interesting about second-language readers is that a text that is appropriate for a beginning EL does not necessarily equate with a lower grade-level text. In other words, the teacher wouldn't use a kindergarten text instead of a seventh-grade one. Cognitively, the seventh-grade EL would be capable of grasping more complexity and abstract concepts than a kindergartner; it is just that the EL needs more frequent, common, and simpler wording and phrasing in English, supplemented by nonlinguistic representations of the linguistically simplified text. They do not think below their age-appropriate level, but are in process of acquiring English proficiency.

Then why not just supply the fully translated text for beginning ELs and avoid the need for unpacking the English text? Well, that depends on the goal of instruction. If the goal is to develop the critical-reading skills in any language, or if it is to simply learn the content of the passage (the story of Frederick Douglass's life as a part of American History) then providing translations in the students' native language (for example, French or Chinese) would be appropriate. Of course, that would be best accomplished where the classroom teacher is fluent in the native language of the beginning EL, or at schools with bilingual or dual-language education programs. This is not always possible, though, given the number of ELs at a particular school or an individual EL's native language. Spanish support would be more available than Akan (spoken in the Ivory Coast), for example. On the other hand, if the goal is to develop an EL's listening, speaking, reading, and writing proficiency in English and of academic disciplines, then it is important that the student have adequate exposure to and practice with texts that are slightly above (not worlds above) the learner's current English proficiency. That way the focus can be on the wording and phrasing to convey meaning, made comprehensible through explanation and concrete examples provided in level appropriate English. The amount of unpacking required for ELs should be more like that of a gift inside a wrapped box than a semitrailer's contents from a cross-country move.

Beyond Beginning English Learners

Every EL's goal is to become a former EL. That may be true, but technically, does anyone who learned a second language ever really stop learning the language (one could make that argument for first languages as well)? If an EL is defined as someone whose native language is other than English and who, as a result of being a nonnative speaker, struggles with learning in English-speaking classrooms because of her listening, speaking, reading, or writing skills in English, then at some point one would expect that the learner would develop English proficiency at a level to participate in classroom instruction like non-English learner students. Although there are some characteristics of ELs that may persist beyond their exiting categorization as ELs, such as accentedness or certain persistent morphological or syntactic errors, once English learners have achieved a level of English proficiency to be exited, they tend to benefit from the same types of language and literacy scaffolding that other students need. Persisting characteristics are common for those who began learning English as older adolescents.

It is important to remember, however, that in addition to their needs in developing English language and literacy skills, ELs possess the immensely valuable asset of bilingualism. Bilingualism gives them a perspective on languages and an additional source of linguistic richness that educators can help ELs capitalize upon. Encouraging all ELs to continue reading all types of texts and writing various types of genres in the native language not only helps promote biliteracy but also fosters a deeper understanding of how the second language works. Ask any foreign-language teacher about how much he ends up teaching English grammar when introducing a grammar point in Spanish or French, and you will understand how much knowledge about one language can help understand and develop another.

SUPPORT FOR INTERMEDIATE AND ADVANCED ENGLISH LEARNERS

Now that the chapter has explored what the opposite ends of the spectrum of developing second-language proficiency look like, it will examine what types of support intermediate to advanced ELs need. Earlier in the chapter it was established that at the beginning levels, the *something more* that ELs need is very extensive, meaning that the text and speech they are exposed to and are expected to produce should ideally be leveled to their current proficiency in English. On the other end, exiting and exited ELs benefit primarily from the same sorts of support that native speakers need, with minor adaptations for specific instances of nonnative language behaviors (pronunciation and grammatical variations from native speaker norms). What lies between these poles is a finer gradation of specialized support for English learners, ranging from the greatest need for EL-specific differentiation at the intermediate level, to a gradually decreasing need for EL-specific differentiation at the advanced level.

It is helpful to look at another example from the CCSS, this time for an intermediate EL in ninth grade who may be reading this passage in social studies or in language arts. The CCSS lists *Farewell Address (1796)* by George Washington as a grades 9–10 appropriate informational text. The following is the first four sentences of the first paragraph:

Against the insidious wiles of foreign influence (I conjure you to believe me, fellow-citizens) the jealousy of a free people ought to be constantly awake, since history and experience prove that foreign influence is one of the most baneful foes of republican government. But that jealousy to be useful must be impartial; else it becomes the instrument of the very influence to be avoided, instead of a defense against it. Excessive partiality for one foreign nation and excessive dislike of another cause those whom they actuate to see danger only on one side, and serve to veil and even second the arts of influence on the other. Real patriots who may resist the intrigues of the favorite are liable to become suspected and odious, while its tools and dupes usurp the applause and confidence of the people, to surrender their interests.

The CCSS Reading Standards for Informational Text Grades 9–10 specify that the student should cite strong and thorough textual evidence to analyze explicit and inferential points made; determine the meaning of figurative, connotative, and technical words and phrases used and their influence on meaning and tone; and delineate and evaluate the argument and claims. In addition to understanding the historical context and who Washington was, ELs need assistance with the language itself, similarly to native speakers and with *something more*.

For an intermediate EL, who understands and uses short sentence patterns with growing complexity and repetitive grammatical structures, disciplinary vocabulary, and idioms and words with multiple meanings, being able to extract meaning from the ninth-grade text in English would require a significant amount of scaffolding. To complicate matters somewhat, even though the hypothetical ninth-grade EL is at a higher level of proficiency than the hypothetical seventh-grade EL, the ninth-grade text is more challenging, so the increase in the EL's proficiency is mitigated by the increase in text complexity. However, because the intermediate EL has much more language knowledge and skill to work with, the *something more* beyond the scaffolding provided for all students will not be as extensive as what would be needed for the seventh-grade beginning EL.

This type of passage would be comprehended more efficiently by native speakers and ELs if the teacher chunked or segmented the passage and supported comprehension in small, understandable portions. In the case of intermediate ELs, the ability to recognize and comprehend relative clauses is developing, so that the immense unpacking and translation required for a beginning EL would be far less for the intermediate EL. The first sentence could be chunked and vocabulary instructed in context for all students as follows:

Against the *insidious wiles* of foreign influence	Teacher, ". . . wiles means?"
(I *conjure* you to believe me, fellow-citizens)	Teacher, "I ask you . . ."
the jealousy of a free people *ought to be* constantly awake,	Teacher, ". . . should . . ."
since history and experience prove that	Teacher, "because . . ."

foreign influence is one of the most   Teacher, "A word for *foes*?"
baneful foes of republican
government.

Issues of difficulty for an intermediate EL with this passage include:

- Unusual sentence structure—the subject of the first sentence, *the jealousy of a free people*, is buried between a relative clause and a parenthetical insertion. This would need to be pointed out for native speakers as well.
- Unusual general academic vocabulary, such as *insidious*, *wiles*, *conjure*, *baneful*, *foes*. Again, these terms would need instruction for most native speakers.
- Use of modal auxiliary verbs—this is an area of difficulty for ELs at the intermediate level. *Ought to be* would require explanation and clarification in terms of other similar modals, such as *should be, must be, has to be*, and so on. Clarification of this modal may not be necessary for native speakers.
- Use of *since* to mean *because*—intermediate ELs might only know *since* in its use as a time marker and not as an alternative way to express *because*.

The pace of unpacking and the portion of the text that is unpacked for ELs would ideally be slower and smaller than for native speakers, but much of the scaffolding for native speakers would also benefit intermediate ELs. The additional scaffolding necessary for ELs at intermediate levels could be provided by the classroom teacher or could be coordinated for the ELD teacher to provide. As can be seen in Table 5.1, the text and language complexity for an advanced EL are approximating those of a proficient native speaker, with specific areas of support required on a less frequent basis than for intermediate ELs.

CULTURAL CONSIDERATIONS

In addition to the continuum of acquiring English proficiency, the EL's culture provides a lens through which he understands what is being learned. While the authors are addressing culture as a lens through which ELs view texts, all students and educators have a culture through which they view content. In addition to language background, the culture includes region of the United States, type of area in which learners live (urban, suburban, rural), family structure, religion, lifestyle, or other experiences that bear on learning. Effective educators are sensitive to the cultural diversity of all students and the challenges that this diversity represents and strategize appropriately.

Recently, the authors were in an urban high school that has a large population of students whose families had immigrated from Haiti. In addition to lacking proficiency in English, some students had not been in school for several years prior to enrollment in this high school. Resources to support their first language, Haitian Kreyól, were not readily available nor were teachers proficient in both the students' first language and academic content, except for one chemistry teacher.

In this high school, a group of first-year teachers were sharing that their biggest challenge was teaching difficult concepts to the Haitian students who did not understand the words in English and they did not know how to communicate in the students' language. They described modeling what was expected, showing visuals, and demonstration labs in science and mathematics for concrete concepts. What seemed to be insurmountable was to teach abstract concepts, like cause and effect. The chemistry teacher had immigrated from Haiti as a ninth-grader himself and shared insight to develop greater awareness among his fellow teachers. The culture of some supports the belief that what happens is willed by a higher being and not in control of the person. Furthermore, cause and effect are not taught in schools. As a collaborative colleague, he went on to offer to meet with the students to help them understand cause and effect as a language arts benchmark so that the ELA teachers could assist the students in being successful with this important and measured benchmark.

LEARNING SCALES AND ENGLISH LEARNERS

It is important for ELs to understand and work toward the same rigorous learning targets as native speakers, even though it will take them more time and, depending on proficiency level, a different route. Learning a second language is a fairly sequential process that takes time, so try as one may, one cannot make a beginning seventh-grade EL write an essay in English that is comparable to those of her native-speaking proficient peers. The best instance of instruction and scaffolding cannot make second-language proficiency appear suddenly out of nowhere. However, appropriate instruction can accelerate the process and lead to higher levels of proficiency, so the key is to provide appropriate instruction given the context in which an EL is taught. When the EL is mixed among a majority of native speakers, the degree to which language, literacy, and academic discipline instruction for the EL is appropriate depends not only on the individual's needs, but also on those of the other students. There is always a compromise when using whole class instruction when there are mixes of native speakers with ELs.

Recall the discussion of instructional differentiation in Chapter 2, in which differentiation takes the form of different resources, time, and/or intensity. The most feasible affordances of appropriate language, literacy, and academic discipline instruction for ELs, the *something more* that they need, often occurs as instructional differentiation: one-to-one interactions between the teacher and EL and small-group interactions of ELs, with or without the teacher (technology-enhanced instruction can be very beneficial in differentiating). Keep in mind that small-group instruction is a high-effect-size strategy (Hattie, 2009). When these more-targeted forms of instruction occur, they can be greatly enhanced by showing the ELs the scales that native speakers should reach in the lesson, giving the ELs a clear view of the ultimate goal.

To keep the learning scales realistic, the success criteria can be adjusted for the ELs' current level of English proficiency, using the ELPA 21 CCSS adaptations. For example, in the fourth grade, CCSS require students to *determine the meaning of words and phrases in oral presentations and literary and informational text.* According to the CCSS *English Language Proficiency Development (ELPD) Framework,* a level 1 EL in the fourth grade would be expected to: *recognize the meaning of a few frequently occurring words, phrases, and formulaic expressions in simple oral discourse, read-alouds, and written texts about familiar topics, experiences, or events, relying heavily on context and visual aids (including picture dictionaries).* The evidence or success criteria on the Benchmark Scale with Evidence may reflect the expectation for the appropriate level of the EL.

While the success criteria in the scale may be adjusted for the EL student in an academic class, differentiation of the time, intensity, and resources used to support the students' language acquisition in the discipline while learning the disciplinary content is essential. In science, for example, the fourth-grade students may be expected to learn the life cycle of a butterfly. To do so, the students read informational text, view video, practice developing a diagram of the life cycle, and then communicate understanding of the life cycle by writing a paragraph to demonstrate the success criteria. EL students in the class follow the instruction and understand the vocabulary because of the high support provided by the video and oral language support. They also have a link to review the video as many times as needed. Completing the diagram by labeling the steps in the life cycle is also accomplished by the ELs fairly easily. The challenge comes in writing a paragraph that details the steps in the life cycle—the success criteria or expectation to demonstrate proficiency on this learning target. The teacher allows the ELs the option of demonstrating understanding in another manner: completing sentence starters that relate to the proficient level, telling the teacher instead of writing the paragraph, or creating a diagram without support that shows understanding.

Teachers of ELs should always keep in mind two considerations. The first is the ultimate ELA outcome the EL should reach, and the second is the EL's current level of proficiency. All instruction must be aimed at reaching that ultimate level of English proficiency required to be college and career ready, but at any given grade, the EL's current level of proficiency may not enable him to meet ELA proficient expectations and demonstration in the academic disciplines. This does not mean that the teacher should just sit back and wait for second-language acquisition to occur. Although there are no determined timelines for how long it should take each individual, there should be a constant sense of timeliness and forward and upward motion. That persistent, gentle pressure toward the ultimate goal, in the most timely yet realistic manner, should be communicated to the EL and made concrete through short- and long-term learning objectives. With the proper balance between giving the EL adequate time and pushing the EL to tasks with ever-increasing challenge, the risk of plateauing at an intermediate level or remaining a long-term EL should be reduced. When both the teacher and learner have a clear sense of the rigorous goal and a general sense of when it should be reached, both have greater agency in making it reality.

PRACTICAL STEPS FOR LEADERS

- Provide professional learning for all teachers to understand WIDA levels.
- Have high expectations for ELs' academic achievement.
- Monitor data throughout the school year on the ELs' progress.
- Be sure that all who teach ELs have deep disciplinary knowledge, pedagogical expertise, and model excellent English in speaking and writing.

PRACTICAL STEPS FOR TEACHERS

- Provide appropriate options for success criteria in the Benchmark Scales with Evidence.
- Differentiate instruction, but maintain high expectations.
- Expect high level and cognitively complex thinking.
- Be sure to add *something more*.
- Provide fluent English models either in real time or via digital resources.

USEFUL ACADEMIC LANGUAGE

EL—English learner whose native language is not English.
Native speaker—Native English speaking student.
Something more—The additional support, strategy, or assistance an EL should have to advance in learning English and in meeting the expectations of CCSS.

Chapter Six

Under-resourced Students

Achieving mastery of Common Core State Standards (CCSS) is a rigorous, yet attainable goal for students, but for the under-resourced student success can seem out of reach. Who are under-resourced students? Under-resourced students may appear lethargic or unmotivated due to lack of sleep or lack of adequate nutrition. Perhaps their academic backgrounds have gaps due to periods of being out of school for moves from one location to another (example: migrant families, employment, or eviction). For some under-resourced students their learning is further hampered due to their families' lack of education or perhaps lack of proficiency in English (discussed in Chapter 5). As the reader can see there are multiple factors outside of school that may affect under-resourced learners. On the other hand, there are under-resourced students who excel until they encounter learning tasks that require contributions that their family or caregivers cannot provide. This chapter addresses how to provide for the success of these students specifically by leading and teaching to control in-school and in-classroom factors, but the strategies and suggestions will be helpful to all learners. Teachers and leaders must understand and recognize the different needs of these students, the adaptations that must be made to accelerate learning, and specific implementation strategies.

Conditions related to living in poverty impact students' learning and may affect under-resourced learners. According to the National Center for Children in Poverty, 22% of America's children live below the Federal poverty line of $23,550 annually for a family of four (Addy, Englehardt, & Skinner, 2013). Families who live in urban centers have an almost 20% poverty rate when compared to suburban areas that have less than 8% families in poverty (Gallagher, Goodyear, Brewer, & Rueda, 2012).

Under-resourced does not mean only lack of family financial assets, but can bring to mind any educationally related resources. Other assets that may be absent are in the areas of physical and nutritional, mental health, and social services. There are many factors beyond the school that affect learning of under-resourced students: cultural roots, community and school context, and interpersonal ones, such as how they cope with adversity (Gallagher et al., 2012). Teachers should develop an awareness of classroom factors they can affect and leaders should develop an awareness of school factors that they can address for success with CCSS and beyond.

SCHOOL FACTORS THAT LEADERS CONTROL

Second to the teacher, the principal has the greatest influence on student achievement with a .36 effect size (Hattie, 2009). The principal's responsibility is to lead to enhance the factors that can be controlled for positive experiences and minimize those that relate to interferences or hindrances to learning. When principals are instructional leaders—that is, they attend to the content of this text and expect research-based curriculum, instruction, and assessment and monitor that they take place—the effect size grows to .66 (Hattie, 2009).

School Culture

Everyone who walks in a school can describe the school culture in a short amount of time. School culture is how we do things around here. It is how visitors and families are greeted and treated along with how administrators treat students and teachers, and how teachers treat students. It is the responsibility of the principal to create a culture focused on student learning with everything else being secondary to that purpose. When the culture is focused on student learning and not for adult convenience, student achievement increases (Taylor, 2010).

Part of the culture and school factors is how students are scheduled, the curriculum, and instruction that is expected. Consider which courses, disciplines, or students are prioritized for in the scheduling process for the next school year. The authors have worked in schools where band and weight lifting were scheduled first, followed by athletic coaches' classes, Advanced Placement classes, and classes for gifted learners. They have also worked in schools where the nonproficient students' classes were scheduled first and the rest of the schedule revolved around accelerating their learning to bring them to proficiency.

A high-school principal who is well known personally to the authors takes pride in hand scheduling all of the nonproficient readers to be sure their academic needs are met, before she allows the registrar and counselors to schedule the remaining 2,000 students. Knowledge of curriculum and instruction along with demonstrations of personal involvement with these important components of the school culture are characteristics of principals who are effective in improving student learning.

Another important concept is how access to excellence is made available or restricted. Are the arts (music, art, piano, dance) available to all students? In one of the local high schools a respected dance instructor provides dance lessons at the school within the school day for those who have prior background and pay a fee of over $100 for the required garment and shoes. This is an example of controlling access to excellence.

An example of open or controlled access to excellence that may be more common is the restriction of admission to honors or advanced classes to those students whom the class teacher believes have the ability to perform well in those classes. In schools where there is open access to Advanced Placement courses for any student who wants to put forth the effort, there is an increase in enrollment and an increase in students who score a three and above on the exam, but the teacher has to teach differently since students have a broader range of backgrounds than when access to excellence is restricted.

Rewards and Sanctions

Evidence of what is important in a school is what is visibly rewarded and what is sanctioned. When the school displays academic banners and trophies beside the athletic and extracurricular trophies, then learning is at least as important as outside-of-school activities. Does the high-poverty school have a debate team similar to the high-socioeconomic-level community high school? In fact, are students on the debate team provided appropriate and attractive clothing to wear to competitions just as they are provided for athletic teams? Going further, do the teams in high-poverty schools wear the same up to date and quality athletic wear of those in a high-socioeconomic-level high school? Another and perhaps more important question is: Are under-resourced students in high-socioeconomic-level schools provided the resources needed and the same expectations as those provided to their middle-class peers by their families?

A telling example is one of the outstanding principals in the authors' community who vowed that the school's student athletes would not be embarrassed by their uniforms when playing teams across town! Nor would she allow a student to be taken off the basketball team for missing practice when his family moved into a nearby motel after the foreclosure of their home and loss of transportation. As this principal told the coach, "There are many students who have no excuse and should be taken off the team for missing practice, but for this student staying on the team and playing in the tournament may change his life." Make decisions in the best interest of students and not for adult convenience.

Academic Resources

Providing academic resources may mean tangible ones, like digital resources, or may be time or intellectual academic support. There are many instances when the assumption is made that students have the resources needed to successfully complete learning tasks, when in fact they do not. The commitment to provide resources cannot be one that is voiced, but one upon which action is taken. Decisions within the school budget, extracurricular budget, and perhaps to seek grants or resources from community businesses or philanthropies has to be considered.

An example from the author's life that has influenced her leadership relates to access to band class. When in junior high school, all of the author's friends were in the band. She wanted to be in the band too, but would not ask her parents to purchase an instrument. To be fair to the parents, readers should know that they were not given the opportunity to make arrangements for use of an instrument. Like many under-resourced students, the 12-year-old assumed the expense was not a possibility. Fast forward 25 years and the author is a middle-school principal in an urban, high-poverty, high-crime community. She and the teachers agreed that no learning task or opportunity would be out of reach for these middle-school students due to finances or education of the parents. Anyone who wanted to be in band was provided an instrument and any student who wanted to perform was given appropriate clothing. They were also taught, modeled, and practiced appropriate language, manners, and behavior for participating in or attending out-of-school events.

Resources for completing projects or other learning tasks were available to students and teachers. The library began to have extended hours before school, after school, and on weekends so the students and families could access the books and other resources within.

The same decision making can be applied to providing college entrance exam preparation, exam fees, and time within the school day to take the exams. Assistance with completion and providing for fees relates to college applications, and not just announcing their availability. Time within the school day should be provided for students to work with their counselors to complete the college applications (and fees if needed), to apply for financial aid, and if needed, transportation for interviews for college entrance and scholarships.

CLASSROOM FACTORS THAT TEACHERS CONTROL

One of the first classroom factors to be addressed and developed to meet all students' needs is to build a relationship of mutual respect between the teacher and the student. Building the classroom into a community of learners where students feel free to learn and take risks with their learning is an important foundational step to any teaching. The authors have seen teacher classrooms where rules and procedures are developed primarily by the students with minimal input from the teacher. These classrooms build a strong sense of efficacy and confidence in the learner, which can contribute to a feeling of safety for the brain to optimally learn.

Specific strategies are displaying student work and minimizing displays of teachers' personal items that are off limits to students, such as personally or financially high-value items. Creating a respectful and inviting atmosphere for teaching and learning means that it is clean, orderly, and predictable; a factor that can be easily put into place immediately. When students enter a classroom, they should feel as if it is where they belong, not that the classroom solely belongs to the teacher, but is student owned. For under-resourced students who often lack stability at home, predictability can develop trust, which can be a key factor in allowing the brain to focus on learning.

Collaboration

One of the challenges with CCSS implementations is the expectation of student collaboration. Often, under-resourced students have an underdeveloped oral language from home and may have been underdeveloped at school as well. As teachers shift from a teacher-centered classroom to a student-centered classroom, this challenge surfaces. In a CCSS classroom, one would expect to see students interacting with knowledge, presenting claims, debating, reading aloud, and engaged in learning tasks that involve oral language. (Recall Chapter 3, Academic Language.) Teachers unfamiliar with the unique challenges of under-resourced students may expect them to be able to engage in these tasks with minimal or no direction. Those same teachers may be surprised when assigning collaboration does not go according to plan. Collaboration, just as any learning task, must be scaffolded through teaching and modeling before moving to guided practice.

Recently, in a high-school the teacher directed students to turn to a shoulder partner and share what was written on their bell work. Several students turned to each other and without saying a word, exchanged papers, read the papers, and gave them back. In debriefing the observation the teacher was frustrated and expressed that she thought students did not want to work together. Her interpretation was that they did not want to work together, when in reality they did not know what she meant for them to do when directed to share. What might seem like a lack of desire might really be a lack of skill. It takes specific skill to express ideas and listen to other ideas. A better approach to this same expectation would be for the teacher to model with another student what sharing the paper would look like before directing students to do so. Additionally, the teacher could have provided sentence stems or question stems to prompt students to share.

Collaboration amongst students must be directly taught and modeled like any other management or learning process in the classroom. For under-resourced students who may not practice these skills outside the classroom, many opportunities for practice without punishment and redirection will be needed in order to experience sustained success in the classroom. Teachers should not give up when challenges arise, but rather keep teaching and reviewing the procedures for the interaction. Teaching students to interact and respond in appropriate manners around content must be explicitly taught, modeled, and practiced every day in the classroom.

Project-based Learning

Another CCSS and higher-level learning task that can be challenging for under-resourced students is project-based learning. Projects have been assigned in science, social studies, language arts, and mathematics classrooms with a myriad of purposes over the years. Readers have seen and even experienced personally and with students meaningful projects as learning tasks that lead to deeper disciplinary understanding. The opposite is also true if the students' success is dependent upon parental support either financially or educationally. The success criteria or grading rubric for a project should be carefully devised to focus on substance and evidence of learning, and not appearance related to the students' financial resources. As one student shared, "Just thinking about a teacher assigning the science or social studies project gives me a headache. I know that I will not do well because I don't have the things it takes and don't have a way to get them. On other work I am a good student." The project-based learning experience can be interesting and motivating for students when options for success exist that consider the under-resourced students. If possible, essential materials should be provided at school. This contributes toward leveling the field for students who do not have access to transportation or funds to purchase materials needed.

Under-resourced students may have particular difficulty with planning a long-term project; they may need assistance with developing a plan with a timeline (scaffolding) that has checkpoints to be sure that they are on track for completion. Provide a template for planning the project and creating the timeline with checkpoints on which the teacher should provide feedback as with any student work. Planning is a skill to be taught and can prevent the students being surprised with a disappointing grade. It would be a misconception to think that under-resourced learners should be excused from the project or any work. Rather, supports should be built in to the learning process from which all students will benefit. The ultimate goal for a project is learning, always keep that in mind.

Research

Implementation of CCSS should result in increased research in and outside the classroom. One elementary teacher was observed using the following strategy for developing a research paper.

First, students took a file folder and glued six envelopes on the inside. Each envelope was labeled and had three blank index cards within. This project was about a specific time period in history, so envelope labels consisted of categories such as culture, food, clothing, government, and so on.

Second, the students wrote the numbers one through three on the outside of each envelope. As the students researched related to the categories, they wrote the facts on index cards, recorded the bibliographic information, and placed the index card in the corresponding envelope, followed by marking through one of the numbers on the outside of the envelope.

When all envelopes had three cards each, the research was complete and the student organizing the research was instructed to write a paper. The contents of each envelope became a paragraph. This strategy can be modified and adjusted according to the age and grade level of the student, but is a useful strategy across grade levels and disciplines for making the process of research concrete.

Resilience

Readers should keep in mind that being under-resourced does not mean being without ability. Many under-resourced students become presidents, school leaders and principals, lawyers, physicians, university professors, and otherwise contribute to society. What sets these successful previously under-resourced learners apart is that they develop resiliency. Resilient people make positive adjustments to negative conditions (Gallagher, et al., 2012). In the case of the under-resourced learner, the negative condition could be homelessness, high mobility, lack of nutrition, lack of adequate health care, or the need to care for siblings or family members. All detract from his or her own academic responsibilities.

Resilience is something that teachers and leaders can influence. By providing students opportunities for competence building either academically, athletically, or socially they are helping them to develop a positive self-esteem. Self-esteem is directly related to academic achievement and future success. Related to competence building and developing a positive self-esteem, is the scaffolding of learning tasks, teachers' feedback to students, and students' self-monitoring of their progress toward mastery. When teachers and leaders strategize to implement the concepts within this text they will assist students in being successful on CCSS and will help them to develop resilience.

Through self-esteem building, students will believe they can be successful and therefore put forth more effort. When they put forth more effort they are successful, even if not at first. Resilient students try again until they get the correct understanding or response and most likely monitor their own progress. Students who are less resilient are more hesitant to take the academic risk of trying if they do not believe that they have a success trajectory. The end result is that the students believe that they have influence and control over their success, even if it is just in school. Those who are successful in school through their efforts to achieve the teachers' high expectations and not lessened expectations will be successful beyond Pk–12 experiences.

RESPONSIBILITIES OF TEACHERS AND LEADERS

The authors believe strongly in the need to maintain rigorous expectations for all students. This chapter is not a discussion about lowering standards for students; rather it is about providing practical steps that can be taken to meet the needs of under-resourced and all other students in schools and classrooms. While students come with unique and specific needs, teachers should resist the temptation to modify content. Adaptations in the school and classroom environment, teaching strategies, and strategies taught to students for developing organization and self-management can lead to success. Do not lower expectations for students, but meet them where they are, using techniques and strategies to accelerate them beyond their own expectations.

The authors have observed challenges in learning that may be related to a lack of family resources. These challenges can be dealt with and overcome in the classroom with a willing teacher who uses specific strategies. Personally, many teachers have not experienced some of the hardships and barriers that students encounter every day. While teachers and leaders cannot solve out-of-school factors, it is their responsibility to control what goes on inside the classroom and the school. Professional learning specifically addressing the needs of under-resourced learners, adaptations needed in the classroom, and strategies to carry out those adaptations to teach under-resourced students should be intentional and purposeful and is the principal's responsibility. (Examples of models or effective professional learning are found in Chapter 8.)

PRACTICAL STEPS FOR LEADERS

- Create a school culture focused on all students learning at a high level.
- Develop systems to support students with learning resources essential to be successful on learning tasks and developing readiness for college and careers.

- Provide access to excellence for all students.
- Provide professional learning that addresses needs, adaptations needed, and useful strategies for teachers.
- Provide materials and digital resources for students for project-based learning and research.
- Provide collaboration time for teachers to discuss specific student needs, adaptations needed in the classroom, and strategies for those adaptations.

PRACTICAL STEPS FOR TEACHERS

- Build relationships of mutual respect with students by creating a student-centered classroom culture.
- Directly teach procedures for collaboration and interaction in the classroom.
- Teach, model, and practice collaboration and interaction daily with students using academic and in-school language.
- Teach specific strategies for planning, organizing, and self-managing, and provide frequent feedback on the plans and progress.
- Teach specific strategies for research and projects, providing equal access and opportunity for all students to engage in this type of learning task.
- Develop resiliency in students through communication that you believe in their potential.

USEFUL ACADEMIC LANGUAGE

Under-resourced—A student who lacks the resources needed for success in the school environment.

Adaptation—The act or process of adapting to meet the needs of students.

Chapter Seven

Clear Goals for Student Self-monitoring and Teacher Feedback

In contrast to the practice of teachers designing instruction on topics that they enjoy, this text emphasizes being purposeful and deliberate in designing instruction based on standards or benchmarks, learning targets, or learning intentions. Selected benchmarks should be those important for ongoing success in school, for college and career readiness, and/or for success on assessments that impact students' futures. Just as careful selection of the benchmark is important, it is just as important how the benchmark, instructional strategies, and success criteria are communicated to students. Students need to understand these components with the same clarity as the teacher.

Chapter 2 addressed instructional planning in which the first step is the selection of the learning target and the success criteria. Checking for understanding and providing timely and specific feedback were also discussed. Chapter 3 addressed academic language and Chapter 4 focused on rigor, including thinking and text complexity. Understanding of these chapters is prerequisite to Chapter 7. This chapter builds on these previous chapters and provides a systematic process for inclusion of these components and to increase student success through the development and implementation of Benchmark Scales with Evidence.

CLEAR GOALS, SELF-MONITORING, AND FEEDBACK

John Hattie (Hattie, 2009) reviewed a plethora of empirical research and conducted meta-analysis arriving at effect sizes (statistical measure that indicates the probability of improved learning) for particular instructional strategies and student-learning processes. He identified that when students have clear goals that they understand, they are more likely to achieve them. Clear goals have a .56 effect size, which means that when a teacher assists students in understanding the expectation, there is a 56% probability of increased learning (Hattie, 2009). Hattie (2009) also communicated that students' self-monitoring of their progress toward achieving goals has a .64 effect size. When you consider that feedback, as described in Chapter 2, has an effect size of .73, and if feedback were to be combined with clear goals and self-monitoring, it is reasonable to hypothesize that learning would improve (Hattie, 2009; Taylor & Watson, 2013).

The authors reflected upon this research while facilitating teachers' collaborative instructional planning as a follow-up to class visits. Part of the instructional plan development included the school district requirement of developing learning scales, which had the intent of students' self-monitoring of their progress toward achieving the benchmark. These were 5-point generic learning scales based on the work of Marzano (2007). The lowest level was 0 (I can't do the work even with assistance), 3 (no major errors), and the highest 4 (application or in-depth learning) (Marzano, 2007).

Generally, teachers posted similar generic learning scales in their classes and from time to time asked students to rate themselves based on these scales. Students and teachers were compliant with this expectation, but did not believe that taking time to use the scales was improving students' learning. In fact, the authors observed and teachers voiced that students indicated at the introduction that they were already at benchmark level (3), because they believed that is what their teachers wanted to hear and they did not want to indicate that they did not achieve a level, even with assistance. The conclusion was that these generic scales were not assisting in achieving the intentions of providing clear goals and student self-monitoring.

BENCHMARK SCALES WITH EVIDENCE

Their in-context research and understanding of the power of clearly understood goals and success criteria, student self-monitoring, and teacher feedback provided the authors with parameters for designing the Benchmark Scales with Evidence (Taylor & Watson, 2013). An example is provided in Figure 7.1 and it would be helpful to view it along with the description. While context, academic discipline, benchmarks, curriculum, and school district expectations may call for adjustments to the Benchmark Scale with Evidence, teachers will find this model to assist them in improving student learning.

The clearly understood goal is represented by the description in each level in the scale. The evidence/success criteria cell for each level provides students with success criteria that will be provided to demonstrate proficiency

Level	Description	Acceptable Evidence Success Criteria
4	Analyze ways the author used comparison and contrast across texts.	Demonstrate critical analysis across texts citing textual evidence in at least one 7-sentence paragraph.
3 Benchmark, Target	Compare and contrast elements in multiple texts.	Chart comparison and contrast across texts using a T-chart or other graphic organizer.
2	Compare and contrast elements within a single text.	Complete comparison and contrast graphic organizer.
1	Identify comparison and contrast within a text.	Point out comparison and contrast in a text.
Entry	Define compare and contrast.	Orally, give the definition of compare and contrast.

Figure 7.1.   ELA Benchmark Scale with Evidence. Created by Melissa Hancock.

for that level. With specificity in these two cells, students can self-monitor their progress toward reaching the learning target or benchmark, Level 3. At the same time, teachers have created concrete evidence on which to provide students feedback. The example, Figure 7.1, is an English Language Arts (ELA) Benchmark Scale with Evidence designed by Melissa Hancock, high-school literacy coach in collaboration with reading teachers.

The first step in designing the Benchmark Scale with Evidence is to select the standard, benchmark, or learning target and write it in the Level 3 description space. This level in the Benchmark Scale with Evidence is always for independent demonstration with on-grade-level texts, not for guided practice. Students are assessed independently so the learning target or benchmark is always an independent demonstration.

Be sure to maintain the rigor of the benchmark, even if the language is simplified to make it clear and concise. Rigor of the benchmark is indicated by verbs, such as *analyze, summarize, identify, evaluate, examine*, and *explain*. If the benchmark has several components it might be best to have the most rigorous component at Level 3 and the less rigorous, but prerequisite components at Level 1 or 2. An example would be the learning target, identify figurative language and analyze how it contributes to tone. Identify (Level 1) would be less challenging than analyze (Level 3), but essential as a prerequisite to analyze.

The second step is writing the acceptable evidence to the right of the benchmark. Ask yourself, "What are the success criteria or acceptable evidence for demonstration of proficiency with this learning target?" Common Core State Standards (CCSS) is about doing and demonstrating, not knowing. Evidence is what you hear or see like partner reading, worked problems, writing, lab demonstration, and so on. Evidence should align with the rigor of the benchmark. For the benchmark, *Identify figurative language and analyze how it contributes to tone*, Level 3 evidence may be a seven-sentence paragraph explaining how specific textual examples of figurative language impact the tone.

The third step is to determine the logical progression of check points from the entry point or lesson introduction to the benchmark. The prerequisite description and acceptable evidence for students' learning and demonstrating of learning outcomes are added for Levels 2, 1, and Entry. Levels 2 and 1 may be collaborative and during guided practice. The lowest level is most probably accomplished during the introduction of the instruction while building and accessing background knowledge essential for moving forward with learning.

When reviewing Figure 7.1 you will notice that the lowest level is written in the positive terms of Entry Level or the Beginning. The authors noticed that when a zero was at the lowest level, students thought it meant *they were a zero* and it seemed to hinder students' progress; therefore, teachers deleted the zero level. As a result the authors have replaced zero with Entry Level.

The last step is to complete the description and evidence for Level 4 or above benchmark. This level is for those students who have greater background knowledge or who achieve the benchmark at a more rapid rate. Level 4 is not intended for everyone and should not be presented as the target. It is for individual differentiation upward. Deeper understanding, higher-level thinking, greater complexity, or foreshadowing of the next benchmark would be appropriate for Level 4. An example of increased complexity would be comparing or analyzing across texts if the learning target had been to compare or analyze within one text. As Koedinger, Corbett, & Perfetti (2012) recommend, proficient students need to delve more deeply and thoughtfully. They do not need more of the same practice.

Once this scale is designed, take Figure 2.1 Scaffold Instruction and rotate it with the apex of the triangle pointing upward and the base or short side at the bottom. You will see a relationship between scaffolding student learning from whole-class introduction to independence with Entry Level to Level 3 in the Benchmark Scale with Evidence. In Figure 7.1, the ELA scale begins with the introduction and students orally defining compare and contrast, followed by identifying, and then comparing and contrasting within one text. Next, at benchmark level the student compares and contrasts across texts by completing a graphic organizer. Above benchmark level is a paragraph analysis of how the author used the elements across texts, which requires more extensive, precise, and accurate language and deeper thinking than completing a graphic organizer. By taking time to design the scale in this way, a logical sequence of instruction that scaffolds students to independence is planned.

Levels and evidences do not represent all of the instruction, but are instructional decision points or check points. The evidences at each level represent the decision point for either intervening and reteaching or moving onward toward benchmark. Without fail, the first time teachers go through this process, they conclude that once scales are designed in this manner they have created the framework for their instructional plan. Unlike the way they may have designed instruction previously, they have designed the evidence of proficiency *first* instead of last and the evidence is not a test or quiz. By making instructional intentions and expected learning outcomes transparent, they have also designed a tool for students' self-monitoring of progress, and for giving feedback to students resulting in effective instruction and increased student learning.

Teachers have shared that their instructional plans are more detailed, making their classroom instruction easier for them to implement and the learning easier for the students. Furthermore, when their principals or other administrators ask about students' progress and how they know the students' progress, teachers can communicate confidently, supported by classroom evidence. The same evidence provided to students and administrators is helpful when meeting with parents. Alicia Michele Nicholson, literacy coach at Ocoee Middle School, summed up the value in using Benchmark Scales with Evidence.

> The academic language used in evidence/artifact portion of the scale now serves as our common language for progress monitoring. By providing our students with copies of the scales for inclusion in their Advancement Via Individual Determination (AVID) binders, students have a running record of their progress and parents/guardians have access to this informative tool. Now, the cornerstone of any conference is each content area's scale. They are living documents which speak to our school's instructional excellence and community-focused transparency.

STUDENT-FRIENDLY SCALES

Teachers have told the authors that scales work best if they are student-friendly. Given that their previous scales may have included negative language, teachers agreed that positive language, rather than deficit language, would affirm and encourage students. Original benchmarks may be written as complex and difficult-to-understand sentences, which created cognitive overload for students. If students have difficulty understanding the scale, they would not have self-efficacy in achieving the learning target. Teachers determined that if needed, the scales should be rewritten in clear and concise statements. It is best to take out unnecessary words, while maintaining the rigor verb and academic language of the benchmark. As one ELA teacher observed when reviewing scales with colleagues, "I think teachers try to impress with a lot of writing to show they are scholarly but students can't understand it." To achieve the stated purpose, the description and acceptable evidence must be written for students' understanding while maintaining the academic language of rigor.

Acceptable evidence or success criteria should be precise to let students know exactly what they have to do to achieve each level. An example is: write a paragraph of no less than five sentences. A nonexample is: write a paragraph or an essay. Mathematics teachers may use a mathematical model or visual to show students what the evidence looks like. Graphic organizers can also be included. The precisely written acceptable evidence does not hinder the proficient students, but provides a clear and achievable target for those less proficient. Readers may want to scan Figure 7.2 that displays benchmark criteria that supports scaffolded instruction and fidelity to the rigor of the learning tasks.

IMPLEMENTATION FOR STUDENT SELF-MONITORING AND TEACHER'S FEEDBACK

There are several queries that teachers should consider to achieve the purpose of the Benchmark Scales with Evidence.

1. How will the teacher assure understanding of the benchmark and evidence/success criteria by students?
2. How will the Benchmark Scale with Evidence assure students' self-monitoring?
3. How will the Benchmark Scale with Evidence facilitate teacher feedback?

Even the best Benchmark Scales with Evidence will not improve learning if not implemented to maximize transparency of the teacher's expectations to students. These scales are used for the period of time the benchmark is being taught, which is most likely several days or even weeks. Students need teachers to review the descriptions of each level at the point of need. Teachers should have taught and modeled for them how to provide evidence for specific levels. Academic language within the descriptions and evidence needs to be taught as described in Chapter 3. The scale is a teaching tool as well as a self-monitoring tool.

Depending upon the resources that teachers and students have, they may implement the tool a little differently. Teachers who have interactive boards show the scale at the beginning of the instructional time and can easily return to it at any time during the class for self-monitoring. As teachers review the

Criteria Description*	Example	Acceptable Evidence Success Criteria	Example
Positive language	Know land forms studied in geography.	Clearly described or shown learning outcome (product)	List 4 land forms. Or, sketch and label 4 land forms.
Ascending rigor from lowest level to benchmark or learning target	If benchmark is analyze, then lower levels may be lower levels of thinking (identify, summarize) or with more support from the teacher or peers.	Aligned to level of rigor of description in each level.	Analyze: Explain in a paragraph of not less than 5 sentences how the author used figurative language to create interest. Cite 3 textual evidences. Identify: Underline & label figurative language in text.
Lowest level is entry point, not a deficit.	Know that geography includes maps with land forms.	Students demonstrate knowledge during the introduction.	Identify land forms on a map.
Scaffold support from lowest level to benchmark or learning target. (See Chapter 2.)	Lowest level is introduction and second level is guided practice. Benchmark level is independent.	May be collaborative until benchmark level, which requires independent demonstration.	In pairs, complete the comparison and contrast graphic organizer. In 5 sentences, compare & contrast 2 strategies for finding the solution.
Above benchmark is more rigorous, or deeper learning, or foreshadows the next benchmark.	Create a digital presentation to teach the relationship of landforms to culture for fifth grade students.	Evidence must be concrete and accomplished independently.	Digital presentation shared with this class and 5th grade students.
Benchmarks with several components may have less rigorous benchmark components and evidence at the lower Levels 1–2.	Identify (Level 1) and analyze impact of literary elements on the main idea (Level 3).	Evidence at each level is aligned with the rigor of that component.	Level 1: Complete the literary elements graphic organizer (identify). Level 3: Select 3 literary elements & explain how each impacts the main idea (analyze). Support your claims with textual evidence.

*Note: The criteria do not represent a hierarchy.

Figure 7.2. Criteria for Scales Aligned with Scaffolded Instruction and Rigor of Learning Tasks.

scales with students, they draw attention to where the students are in their progress toward benchmark level. Perhaps teachers prompt students, "Tell the class what we have accomplished at the Entry Level and Level 1 and share the evidence." By modeling self-monitoring, the teacher helps the students in learning to be explicit with their descriptions of their own progress.

Another model observed to be effective is for each table to have the printed scale within a plastic sleeve for students to use throughout the day. According to teachers, one of the most effective methods is for each student to have her copy of the scale and date with the teacher's initial when evidence for a level has been demonstrated. These may be kept in the student's notebook. When students have digital resources, they may have their individual scales on their devices. This technique provides the teacher an opportunity to give explicit feedback and allows the student to concretely self-monitor progress.

Fred Turner, social studies teacher, collaboratively planned scales with colleagues. For each region in the world studied, the students identify the geography of the region, learn how the geography influences inhabitants' lives, and analyze how the geographic features impacted the civilization's development. These teachers implement a similar scale for each region, building upon the last one but addressing the three concepts that apply to each region. Level 4 is more complex, requiring students to analyze across regions. Fred Turner provided the unsolicited reflection that follows on his expectations related to implementation of Benchmark Scales with Evidence.

> I think what I like the best about it [*sic* Benchmark Scales with Evidence] is
> that it provides automatic differentiation. Students can work at their own pace
> and determine if they want to go past the target. It also helps them feel some
> control over their work as they monitor their own progress. I'm foreseeing that
> by having similar evidence requirements as content changes, students will get
> incrementally more skilled at completing these tasks. (Frederick Turner, Social
> Studies Teacher, Liberty Middle School, Orlando, FL)

The geography scale follows in Figure 7.3. Fred and colleague geography teachers were thoughtful as they refined the Benchmark Scale with Evidence to the context of their curriculum, benchmarks, and students. They changed "level" to "phase" to communicate that learning has phases and that all students have the opportunity to progress through Phase 4. Rigor is scaffolded from Entry through Phase 3, an analysis within one text. Phase 4 is more complex as it is an analysis across texts with an expectation of more writing than in Phase 3. Remember that writing has greater cognitive demand than does speaking.

For student self-monitoring and for the teacher's feedback, readers will see that on the far right of Figure 7.3 there is a column for date completed and initials. This column provides a record for the student and the teacher to provide feedback at the point at which each phase is completed. For this academic discipline, benchmarks are for the course, but this scale is for the learning goal: study of the Mesopotamian region. Therefore, the description is for the learning goal not for the larger benchmark and it will last for several weeks.

Benchmarks:

1. Explain how physical characteristics, natural resources, climate and absolute and relative locations have influenced settlement, interactions, and economies of ancient civilizations of the world.
2. Analyze the relationship of physical geography with the development of the ancient river valley civilizations.

Learning Phase	Learning Goal Description	Acceptable Evidence Success Criteria	Date Completed Initials
Phase 4	Compare and contrast the effects of geography between the Mesopotamian civilizations and the hunter gatherers of the Neolithic Era.	Write three 5-sentence paragraphs comparing and contrasting how geography influenced both sets of people. Include 3 evidences from the text in paragraphs 2 and 3.	
Phase 3 Target	1.Categorize geographic features that influenced the settlement of the Mesopotamian civilizations and influenced the interactions with other peoples and civilizations. 2.Analyze the relationship between physical geography and how the Mesopotamian civilizations developed.	1.Complete a Geography Influence Matrix (GIM). 2.Write a minimum of 5 sentences to explain how Mesopotamia's geography either positively or negatively impacted the people.	
Phase 2	Locate and describe specific geographic features that influenced Mesopotamian civilizations.	1.Label the map with Mesopotamia's geographic features. 2.Choose 2 features and describe their impact on the people.	
Phase 1	Understand how geographic features can influence peoples' lives.	Cause & Effect graphic organizer. Show geography as the cause and its influence as the effect.	
Entry	Identify and define key geographical terms, features, and landforms.	Complete the Frayer Diagrams for each term.	

Figure 7.3. Geography Benchmark Scale. Created by Fred Turner and colleagues.

Algebra teacher Mario Medley believed that the scale was supporting his students' achievement of deeper understanding of their own learning. After the students became proficient with the concept of using the Benchmark Scale with Evidence and it was time to begin a new chapter, Mario asked the students to preview the chapter and identify the benchmarks to be learned and success criteria for mastery. In shared practice, the class developed Figure 7.4 on their interactive white board and Mario saved it for future use and shared with the authors. While this is the first draft of the scale, the students demonstrated that they understood how to develop a scale and how it was to be used.

Mario and his colleagues collaborated to develop the final scale. Mathematics is a precise language so the teachers had some concern about the format of the Benchmark Scale with Evidence as they wanted the success criteria to represent the total expectations of mastery. After some discussion, they agreed that the format seen in Figure 7.1 was exactly what was needed for consistency, but they added a more explicit set of success criteria for each level to the alternate side of the paper that had the standard scale format. Figure 7.5, Quadratic Scale with Precise Evidence, is an example showing the precision that the teachers used for student self-monitoring of progress and for feedback. This mathematics example demonstrates how the scales may be adjusted for context, discipline, and students to be most effective in improving students' learning.

What might a scale for systems of equations look?	Level	Evidence
	0 – I know what a system is.	Gives 3 examples of systems.
	1 – I can identify a solution to a system of equations using a table or graph.	Graph 2 lines and show that their solution is where the lines intersect (cross). Make a table.
	2 – I can do 1 plus solve using substitution	$y = 3x + 2$ $3x + 2y = 12$ } Solve w substitution
	3 – I can do 2, plus solve using elimination.	$3x - 2y = 15$ $2x + 2y = 9$ } Elim.
	4 – I can come up with examples of systems in everyday events.	I can make systems problems from camping or internet use.

Figure 7.4. Classroom Developed Quadratic Scale. Created by Mario Medley's class.

INSTRUCTIONAL DIFFERENTIATION

Teachers who implement Benchmark Scales with Evidence recognize that instructional differentiation is more easily facilitated. As students self-monitor and teachers provide feedback, the evidence is readily available to quickly sit with an individual student or a few who need specific clarifications or more practice. The same is true for those who demonstrate proficiency at each level more quickly than other students as they can be given support to work toward Level 4.

As the acceptable evidence is selected, the learners should be considered. Three teachers may be teaching the same benchmark, but have learners in their classes with varying achievement levels. While the benchmark remains the same, the instructional strategies, time for learning at each level (introduction, guided practice, and independent practice), and acceptable evidence may vary. One class may have less proficient readers and writers; therefore

0- I can recall critical vocabulary of quadratics: axis of symmetry, vertex, max/min, domain/range.		1- I can graph a quadratic function in vertex form. $y= a(x-h)^2+k$	
What does $y = x^2 + 2$ do to the parent function $y = x^2$?	What does $f(x) = -(x-3)^2$ do to the parent function $f(x)=x^2$?	Graph the following: $y=2(x-3)^2 + 1$	Graph the following: $f(x)=-(x+2)^2 -5$
Given a graph, identify key vocabulary on the graph.	Create a Frayer model, in your own words, to explain each of the above words.	Graph the following: $y=-\frac{1}{2}(x+1)$	Describe how vertex form is related to transformations.
2- I can graph a quadratic function in standard form. $y= ax^2 + bx + c$		3- I can solve quadratic equations/systems over the complex numbers. (Find roots, zeros, factors, intercepts.)	
Graph the following: $f(x)= x^2+6x+5$	Graph the following: $y= -x^2 - 3x + 2$	Solve using two different methods. $9 - 4x = 2x^2$	$y=x2-7x-6$ $y=8-2x$
Change to vertex form: $y = 4x^2 - 8x +2$	Create a Venn Diagram comparing and contrasting vertex form with standard form.	Solve using 2 different methods. $x^2 + 8x + 6 = 0$	Compare the methods of solving quadratics to determine the best overall method.
4- I can create a real life scenario where knowledge of quadratics would be relevant.			
Recreate a scenario in the book or apply knowledge of quadratics to a new scenario. Create a technology-based presentation of your scenario, solution, and findings.			

Figure 7.5. Quadratic Scale with Precise Evidence. Created by Mario Medley.

the teacher indicates a five-sentence paragraph as acceptable and spends more time in guided practice. Another class has the students who read and write above proficiency; the teacher may indicate acceptable evidence will be in three paragraphs and moves to independent practice in less time. Also, in the latter class more students may achieve Level 4 than in the former class.

When selecting the acceptable evidence for each level the teacher may choose to indicate options. An option for *identify* may be to underline or list or label. Options for *compare* within one text may be to write a comparison paragraph or to complete a graphic organizer. Or, the choices may have one at the rigor of the description and the other may be a little higher in rigor. In the comparison example, writing the paragraph is more rigorous than completing a graphic organizer. Students are motivated by choice as it empowers them and gives them control over their own learning. By giving choice in how students show what they know and can do, more students will achieve at higher levels.

Exceptional Student Education

Differentiation applies to students with special needs also. Exceptional student education (ESE) requires individual educational plans (IEP) for students served. While the benchmark or learning target should remain the same, accommodations should be provided consistent with the student's IEP. Acceptable evidence may be selected either by the teacher or student and aligned with the IEP. At Level 3 independent demonstration of benchmark proficiency remains, but accommodations of time or resources (e.g., assistive technology) should be consistent with the IEP.

English Learners

Differentiation also applies to English learners (ELs). Teachers of ELs may spend more time early in the instruction on oral language development than a teacher whose students are English proficient. However, teachers of ELs who have implemented Benchmark Scales with Evidence have shared that their students want to learn at Level 4 and that they are motivated to do so. The transparency of the expectations with the success criteria provides students equitable access to excellence, who previously may not have been given higher-level learning opportunities. One novice teacher happily shared, "My English learners worked harder and more achieved Level 4 than my general education students." The ELs achieved higher than the teacher's expectations, showing her that they always could have achieved at higher levels!

MAKE LEARNING ACCESSIBLE

In summary, Benchmark Scales with Evidence make learning accessible to all students. Through transparent instructional expectations and demonstration of proficiency, students' confidence is developed. They are motivated to engage with more challenging tasks as they have some control over their learning. Benchmark Scales with Evidence reflect scaffolded support from high to low support (Level 3) and scaffolded lower to higher levels of thinking and complexity (see Chapter 4). Through collaborative instructional planning and scale development, teachers have more precise instruction and more aligned evidence with benchmark descriptions. With the benchmark description and acceptable evidence shown, teachers indicate that more students and different students are motivated to work toward Level 4 proficiency.

PRACTICAL STEPS FOR LEADERS

- Develop new objective lenses when visiting classrooms and looking for rigor.
- Listen and look for rigorous language used correctly by teachers and students.
- Seek evidence of alignment of the standard, benchmark, or learning target and evidence of student work.
- Support teachers in developing Benchmark Scales with Evidence for student self-monitoring and for teachers to provide explicit and timely feedback.

PRACTICAL STEPS FOR TEACHERS

- Expect all students to achieve proficient level for each benchmark and more students to achieve above proficient for each benchmark.
- Use the same benchmarks or learning targets for all students.
- Differentiate how students achieve the benchmark or learning target.
- Be clear on the evidence or success criteria that demonstrate proficiency and each step toward proficiency.
- Use the scale to differentiate for different learners, including those who achieve above the learning target.

USEFUL ACADEMIC LANGUAGE

Benchmark scale with evidence—Scale designed to make learning intentions and success criteria clear, to provide high expectations for all students, and to support instructional differentiation; aligned with scaffolded instruction and scaffolded rigor.

Effect size—Common measure after conversion to communicate the effect of an application studied.

Learning intentions—Learning target, instructional goal.

Meta-analysis—Research that analyzes the effects across appropriate studies are converted to a common measure for quantification, comparisons, and interpretations (Hattie, 2009, p. 3).

Scale—Rubric for making instructional goals and success criteria clear, and for student's self-monitoring, and teacher feedback.

Success criteria—Acceptable evidence of proficiency or mastery of standard, benchmark, or learning target.

Chapter Eight

Collaboration to Empower Teachers for Success on CCSS

Collaboration is a term educators hear with increasing frequency. Science teachers need to collaborate with reading coaches to improve students' access to science standards-based learning. School leaders need to collaborate with parent and community groups to build capacity for long-term improvement and support at home and in the community for the increased expectations for student learning. Students need to collaborate with each other for support in the learning process. There is a growing consensus that more is accomplished when people work together to leverage their assets, rather than independently. But what does it mean to work together? Is it enough for every individual to do his or her task or job well, coordinating efforts toward a common goal? Or does collaboration ask for more than cooperation alone?

CHARACTERISTICS OF COLLABORATION

Collaboration experts Marilyn Friend and Lynne Cook (2010, p. 7) define collaboration as, "a style for direct interaction between at least two co-equal parties voluntarily engaged in shared decision making as they work toward a common goal." They note six defining characteristics of collaboration. The authors of this text believe that collaborative teams should create ground rules based on these characteristics prior to initiating collaborative decision making.

Collaboration Is Voluntary

Friend and Cook (2010) assert that collaboration is voluntary. Those who take part in collaboration choose to do so. This does not mean that the expectation of collaboration is never mandated. But even when imposed by school policies and procedures, collaboration needs to be consented to by all parties, if it is to be effective. Perhaps you have experienced attempts at collaborating with disengaged colleagues who were present only because they were required to be. These are the times when it seems much easier to work in isolation than with others. Getting from cooperation to collaboration is worth the effort, however.

Parity among Participants

The second characteristic of collaboration Friend and Cook discuss is parity among participants. This means that each person's contribution is valued equally, and that each person's influence is equivalent. Now how can this be if the participants are of different ranks and hold positions of varying responsibility? Surely a principal would wield greater power over the decision-making process than a para-educator. Not necessarily, as a principal may remain neutral and if he cannot do so on a particular topic, then perhaps the collaboration may need a different focus. Although teachers and school leaders may have different degrees of authority in their official positions, when collaborating for a specific purpose, they can establish an environment that values each individual's unique perspective and contribution. No one wants to think that his or her ideas are dismissed or perceived as inconsequential because of perceived status or rank. And, missing the insights of any collaborator could leave a gaping hole in planned actions and solutions. So, every collaborator should believe that he or she could offer the best idea or sharpest analysis, and potential answer to the problem, no matter his job or pay grade. Every collaborator should think the same way about everyone else.

Mutual Goals

Mutual goals are the third characteristic of collaboration that Friend and Cook identify. This quality may seem self-evident, but assumed goals could mean divergent goals. For example, if a group of teachers comes together to collaborate in addressing English learners' (ELs) achievement, the English for speakers of other languages (ESOL) teachers' unspoken goal may be to continue providing sheltered support for the majority of ELs as long as possible while the disciplinary content teachers' goal might be to advance the most ELs from the EL category as soon as possible. Once it is clear that the shared goal of providing the best support for ELs to become sufficiently proficient in English listening, speaking, reading, and writing to achieve at proficient levels in all subjects, collaborators from all disciplines and roles can make explicit what that means to their instruction.

Responsibility

Cook and Friend separate two aspects of responsibility in the fourth characteristic, participation in and decision-making about the collaborative activity. Given the circumstances, there can be two different degrees of responsibility in these elements of collaboration. For example, a reading coach and a kindergarten teacher can be equal partners in coplanning a reading activity, making decisions together given the expertise of both—the coach's knowledge of reading development and the kindergarten teacher's knowledge about her students and the class as a whole. However, in carrying out the activity, both professionals need not participate equally for true collaboration. Depending on the nature of the activity, either collaborator might be the best sole leader, or they both could copresent different parts.

Sharing Resources

Teaching children to share can be challenging. Hopefully educators who need to collaborate were taught well because Cook's and Friend's fifth characteristic of collaboration is sharing resources. Each collaborator should be seen as bringing important resources to the table, ready and willing to share them for the established goal. Resources do not necessarily mean material goods or financial assets. Certainly, they are important to achieve many outcomes, but other intangible resources such as professional relationships are often crucial forms of support. If a teacher has parent volunteers who could be instrumental in meeting a collaborative goal, yet the teacher fails to offer this resource lest the volunteers' time be diverted from another of the teacher's projects, then the teacher lost an opportunity to contribute. If someone is part of a collaborative team and never offers anything of value, others may begin to perceive the member as less valuable.

Shared Accountability

Cook's and Friend's sixth characteristic is shared accountability for outcomes, good and bad alike. If one person does not meet his or her responsibility, and the outcome suffers as a result, all members share blame for the regrettable consequence. Pointing the finger at the one who dropped the ball won't make the result better. This means that everyone is accountable to each other as well as to the outcome. When outcomes are positive, all members should enjoy the ensuing praise and celebration, sharing the accolades for their exceptional teamwork.

IMPROVING STUDENT-LEARNING OUTCOMES

Collaboration is an effective method of improving teacher effectiveness and student-learning outcomes. If clarity in the expected outcome and agreement to the expected outcome are not established first, then the collaboration may not result in better student-learning outcomes.

Collaborative Instructional Planning

One of the most effective collaborative practices is for teachers who teach the same course or standards to plan together, even if they adjust instruction for their unique learners. The first step is to agree upon the standards, benchmarks, or learning targets to be taught in a specific timeframe. Second, agree upon the Benchmark Scale with Evidence as described in Chapter 7. The collaborative group may decide that for different learners resources will vary as will instructional strategies for specific students' learning needs. However, these differences should be grounded in student evidence and supported by the group.

While meeting, the collaborative team should determine the common assessment. Only with a common assessment will the group be able to analyze effectiveness of the plan and the differences in implementation. When one teacher sees the results of another's implementation, the door is opened for continual improvement in this professional group, who are committed to each other's success.

Collaboration on Mini-assessments and Data Analysis

The purposes of mini-assessments are to predict student-learning outcomes as measured by the accountability assessments and to inform instruction. Collaboration among those involved with developing mini-assessments, teaching measured learning targets, and evaluating results of mini-assessments will enhance the intended results.

Inter-Rater Reliability

With the purpose in mind of predicting student-learning outcomes and informing instructional decisions with mini-assessments or on-demand writing, inter-rater reliability has to be established. Inter-rater reliability means that each person in the collaborative team who assigns a score has been prepared with the same mental model of the criteria for a given score. If inter-rater reliability is not established and continually revisited with practice, the scores or mini-assessment results may not be reliable for the intention of predicting and improving student-learning outcomes. While the concept of inter-rater reliability relates to all scoring or grading, the example used herein is for on-demand writing.

If the mini-assessment is on-demand writing then the rubric and criteria for scoring have to be understood and practiced with application to sample papers. If a six-point rubric is used, an anchor paper or example for each level one through six should be provided to create a mental model for each level and for reference. Collaborators should discuss why each paper is scored at each of the levels, rather than at a different level. Next, the participants should be given an unscored sample paper to individually score. After scoring, discussion of the different ratings to increase understanding of each level and to achieve greater inter-rater reliability should take place. If any one participant seems to score quite differently from the others, then the leader (administrator, instructional coach, team leader, etc.) may want to coscore with that participant until greater alignment in scoring is achieved.

Now, the participants are ready to score their students' papers or the papers that have been assigned for them to score. The leader for this experience may select two to three scored papers from each participant's papers and rescore them to see the extent to which the scores are aligned. The random rescoring and comparison, followed by discussion, will assist the leader in achieving inter-rater reliability and meaningful scores within the collaborative group. For predictive outcomes, this process should be repeated for every mini-assessment occurrence, not just the first occurrence that is hand scored.

Analysis of Data to Inform Instruction

Once the papers are scored, the data should be analyzed to inform instruction. The goals of mini-assessments or on-demand writing practice are to increase consistency in teacher effectiveness and to increase student learning in the assessed benchmark or learning target. To measure the goal of increased teacher effectiveness, the range or variance of scores in a teacher's class and within a grade level should be reduced. Rank order each teacher's scores from lowest to highest and compute the mean or average score. In addition to comparing the means, the lead may want to compare the rank order of scores of teachers within a grade to see differences across teachers. The mean score indicates if student achievement has increased. By itself neither the mean nor the variance is enough to determine if teacher effectiveness and student achievement have improved.

An example on a six-point writing rubric would be the range from 1.0 to 3.5 and the mean of 3.0 on the first on-demand writing practice. As the teacher provides specific feedback to students, models writing, and guides students to improve writing, the expectation would be that the range or variance would be reduced and the mean increased in the second on-demand writing. Hypothetically, scores of 1.5 to 4.0 with a mean of 3.5 result on the second on-demand writing practice. The mean has increased, providing initial indication that students have improved in writing but the variance has not been reduced, suggesting that the teacher is not consistently more effective with each individual student. This example is displayed in Table 8.1, Sample Mini-assessment and Data Monitoring, which may provide a beginning point for making data transparent to improve student learning.

One such experience is not enough to draw a conclusion but represents initial evidence. A third and perhaps fourth on-demand writing mini-assessment should take place after informed instruction based on analysis of students' writing. To close the achievement gap and improve student learning, the variance has to be reduced, the lowest scores moved to higher levels, and the mean increased over time. Trends in continual improvement of the mean and reduction in variance over several mini-assessments would be the better evidence to predict student-learning outcome improvements.

Across teachers the same data points should be considered. The variance and mean for each teacher within a grade should be compared to see who is improving the lowest students' learning and pushing the higher-achieving students to even better learning outcomes. Observe teachers' score rankings and see how the scores are clumped together. If a pattern emerges, it may indicate that the teacher has a scoring pattern or a teaching pattern. To determine if the scores reflect instructional expertise, the lead needs to visit the classroom and to determine if the teacher has a pattern of scoring or scores reliably the scored papers should be analyzed.

In one middle school the authors noted that the achievement gap (variance) between EL and general education students was closing and the faculty celebrated their success. On closer inspection the authors noted that the mean scores had dropped and the high end of the scores had lowered over several years, creating a downward trend. In this case, the variance was reduced as was student achievement. It is important to analyze from several data points since it is possible to reduce the variance and close the achievement gap without increasing student achievement. It is also possible to increase the mean (by targeting students who score around the mean and median) but not reduce variance, thus the lowest-performing and most in need students are not impacted.

Equity and access to excellence for all students means that the variance is reduced and the mean increased through consistent effective instruction. This reasoning is why comparisons across teachers of means, variance, and reliability are essential. Ask yourself, to what extent are all students being positively impacted through collaboration involving effective teaching, learning, feedback (based on data and other evidence), and enhanced effectiveness processes?

Teacher	Mini-assessment 1 Variance (1–6)	Mini-assessment 1 Mean (1–6)	Mini-assessment 2 Variance (1–6)	Mini-assessment 2 Mean (1–6)	Notes
1	1.0–3.5	3.0	1.5–4.0	3.5	Slight increase in M and no reduction in Variance. Needs to push higher with 3+ students.
2	1.5–4.0	3.5	1.5–4.0	3.5	No improvement. Check differentiation and feedback to students.

Table 8.1. Sample Mini-assessment and Data Monitoring

Collaborate with Data and Evidence

Once data have been aggregated and charted for a visual representation, the participants should have time to collaborate. On six tables (or as many scoring levels as needed) each teacher should place a representative paper from the ones they scored. After each teacher has placed a representative paper on each table, a jigsaw or other strategy should be used for collaborative discussion of the differences among the criteria met for each level of papers. Collaborators may choose to use sticky notes to make suggestions, ask questions, or note something related to reliability of the ratings. In other words, this is another step toward inter-rater reliability to determine how consistent the scoring was and for the participants to become more expert in scoring the next set of papers.

Following this visual and engaging reflection and learning, the participants should review the data on the students' scores. This second step is essential so that those who have more highly scored papers and whose scores were aligned with the rubric's criteria provide strategies and assistance to those whose scoring was less aligned or whose scores had a lower mean, greater variance, or all three. The scores alone are not indications of more effective teaching nor increased student-learning outcomes and must be balanced with expertise in scoring, resulting in a highly reliable process for predicting student-learning outcomes. Collaborative professional learning among teachers with complex thinking, as is required by those who use this or a similar process, professionalizes their work and focuses on equity and access to excellence for all students.

PROFESSIONAL LEARNING FOR TRANSFER TO PRACTICE

Instead of in-service or workshops, the authors prefer to use the term *profes-sional learning*. Experiences that transfer to improved professional practice are intellectually stimulating; concern new curriculum, resources, research, or data; and include engagement with colleagues. An experience with many, many slides and handouts that only includes lecture does not respect the expertise that is brought to the setting by participants, nor does it require any intellectual engagement or thinking. A positive example would include inter-action among participants and the lead, modeling and practicing with the target learning, and reflection on the learning.

Book Studies

Within schools and across schools, school districts, and borders educators may engage in book studies. There could be a leader who facilitates discus-sions, or each participant may facilitate a chapter discussion. Some schools have school-wide book studies, or a collaborative team may choose one in which they have a particular interest.

Action Research

Action research is a positive example of professional learning during which a data- or evidence-based need has been identified. This data or evidence could be within a classroom, grade, course, discipline, or school. Those who choose to conduct the action research seek out research-based resources or strategies to address the need, implement the strategies, and then share the results. Sometimes it might seem that data or evidence that does not improve learning made the action research invaluable when the contrary is true. It is important to know what does not work better just as it is important to discov-er new strategies and resources that improve learning. The end question should be, "What worked for which students under what condition?"

Data Study

Data study may not sound like professional learning, but it is an excellent and effective practice. A detailed example has been shared related to mini-assess-ments and their use. If the collaborators analyze data objectively by student subgroups, it will become clear for whom the instructional practices are working the best and the least. It can easily lead to instructional differentia-tion and to knowing, not just thinking, that something works well.

An elementary mathematics teacher in a high-poverty school shared that under the previous principal, there were monthly data chats that assisted the school's teachers to focus on the most immediate student needs. When the principal was promoted to a school district position, the next principal did not continue the data-chats practice, resulting in annual reduction in student achievement for four years until he was replaced. Data is objective and not personal. It helps collaborative teams to make informed decisions and should be provided for by principals (Taylor, 2010).

Massive Open Online Courses (MOOCs)

Seldom is professional learning mentioned without a person asking if it is online. There are many available online opportunities for Common Core State Standards (CCSS) topics, issues, or controversies for teachers and administrators, often provided by professional organizations. Most can be accessed for reasonable fees, but some are free such as Massive Open Online Courses (MOOC). Three examples of MOOCs that may be of interest are:

- Common Core in Action: Literacy Across Content Areas, https://www.coursera.org/course/ccss-literacy1
- Common Core in Action: Math Formative Assessment, https://www.coursera.org/course/ccss-math1
- Constructive Classroom Conversations: Mastering Language for the Common Core State Standards (Elementary), https://novoed.com/common-core

Lesson-study Research Teams

Lesson study may be the ultimate in collaborative professional learning, focused on continuous improvement. A misconception regarding lesson study is that the purpose is to create a perfect lesson. Nothing could be more incorrect. The purpose is for the lesson-study research team to collaborate to create a lesson, and for the members of the lesson-study research team to be present either through digital means or on site to gather data related to how students respond to the implementation of the collaboratively designed lesson.

Following the lesson, the research team reflects on what went well and makes edits that may make the lesson implementation better. If time permits, another member of the lesson-study research team will teach the same lesson and then share reflections again. This process can be repeated with each member teaching and the others gathering data. The authors have found lesson study to be effective in assisting implementation of standards-based and research-based instruction with the teachers being empowered with the expectation to commit to each other's success and to improve one's own practice.

LEADERSHIP FOR EFFECTIVE COLLABORATION

The vice president of the authors' local power company shared that in his business, a mistake can have dire consequences for employees and customers. In the power company they have a *culture of active caring* (Taylor, 2010). Leaders and employees are committed to this culture because it means that each is accountable to let colleagues know when they are not performing a task accurately or within the safety measures that they have been taught to use. This culture of active caring means that they expect and provide each other ongoing and continuous feedback. When one provides another with feedback, it may save his life or that of another, just as when one educator provides another feedback it may mean the difference in being effective or ineffective.

School leaders are encouraged to develop a culture of active caring. The school culture will either support or detract from teachers' buy-in to collaboration. First, like the power company's vice president, principals should have a clear vision of professional collaboration and the goal to be achieved. Then, they should clearly communicate and model the expectation. As an example, the vision is that teachers who teach the same course will meet weekly to plan instruction, to design Benchmark Scales with Evidence, and to design common assessments. The goal is for all students to have the most effective instruction and support to master learning targets and for the administrators, teachers, and students to monitor progress toward mastery.

Once the vision and goal are clearly communicated, parameters have to be designed that provide time and a conducive place for the collaborative team. Without a regularly scheduled time and a specific purpose that assists teachers and staff with an immediate positive reinforcement (like students are more engaged), most likely the collaboration will not be effective. Staff members are mentioned since there are para-educators, teacher leaders, and administrators who should also participate. How will the para-educator improve in knowledge and skill if not present and learning from others?

Accountability for participation is essential in the form of notes or agreements, instructional plans, and results of the students' learning shared on the school's intranet or a folder that is available to the collaborative team. If collaboration is important, then administrators and teacher leaders should participate, provide their expert knowledge and coaching, and support implementation of the collaborative team's decisions. By being present during collaboration, if there is a team member who is not engaged or who does not follow up with implementation, then the teacher leader or administrator can intervene with personal knowledge.

Almost any group of administrators and teacher leaders will indicate that they are familiar with professional learning communities (PLCs). If you ask for effectiveness ratings of their PLC from ineffective use of time (0) to excellent use of time and resulting improved student-learning outcomes (5), it is unlikely that you will hear many ratings of 5. While collaboration has been well documented to yield better outcomes than individual effort, PLCs are seldom implemented with parameters that result in these promised results. PLCs most often end up being used to address administrative items. Furthermore, some faculty members do not attend due to other responsibilities, like athletic coaching, child care responsibilities, or other meetings. A PLC or any collaborative group is only as effective as the consistent participation and commitment to the group of the members or it will be viewed as a compliance component of the teacher's professional life and not a help in improving effectiveness.

Recently, the author asked a group of teacher leaders from K–12 about their experiences of effectiveness with a PLC. The consensus was that the effectiveness depends upon the principal.

- Is she engaged with the PLC? Does she follow up on the sessions?
- Does she provide time, space, and resources?
- Does she believe in collaboration to the extent that she also collaborates?

Out of the 22 present in this discussion, one literacy coach shared that the most effective PLC in which she has been a member is the instructional coaches' PLC in her school. She explained that regardless of disciplinary expertise (science, mathematics, social studies, technology, literacy), they all have the same goal of supporting each other in being more effective, believe that they can learn from each other's expertise, and are committed to each other's success. Unknowingly, this literacy coach shared the characteristics of high-performing teams. They share a common goal, possess different expertise, hold each other accountable, and are committed to each individual's success.

LEADING, TEACHING, AND COACHING TO IMPROVE STUDENT-LEARNING OUTCOMES

Along with collaboration, professional learning, and facilitated reflection and empowerment, there is also a role for leaders to coach others to improve student-learning outcomes. Leaders know that it can be difficult to provide authentic coaching feedback to improve professional effectiveness for administrators, teacher leaders, and classroom teachers. All like to hear that they are effective and expert in their professional work, but few invite feedback on how to improve. Whether a teacher leader or administrator, deep knowledge and understanding of effective pedagogy and disciplinary knowledge are important precursors to effective instructional leadership. Instructional leadership, which focuses on explicit expectations for instruction supported by resources and processes for improvement, consistently yields the greatest gains in student achievement when compared to other types of leadership (Hattie, 2009; Taylor, 2010).

The concepts within this text should assist readers with specific strategies and content to incorporate when coaching to improve professional effectiveness. When walking through classrooms take time to provide feedback to teachers, rather than using walkthroughs to demonstrate visibility and to monitor instruction. Grissom, Loeb, and Master (2013) found that principals who took time to provide specific instructional feedback and to have discussions related to resources were associated with greater gains in student learning than those who did not.

Look for scaffolded instruction with consistent checks for understanding and instructional differentiation among students as needed. Suggest to teachers to talk less and listen to students more through facilitated inquiry, and observe how this practice leads to increases in moderate to high levels of thinking and complexity in student-learning tasks. In contrast, generic feedback from leaders, such as *use high-yield strategies*, does not assist in improving instructional effectiveness.

The processes, content, and strategies within this text should support understanding of expectations of CCSS and success with the implementation. Many of the instructional strategies and leadership processes were refined in collaboration with teachers and leaders in diverse urban schools in various grades and disciplines. *Leading, Teaching, and Learning Common Core State Standards* is a professional companion and resource for the journey toward developing students' proficiency through the enhanced effectiveness of leaders and teachers.

PRACTICAL STEPS FOR LEADERS

- Create a culture of active caring (Taylor, 2010).
- Invest in the time and resources needed for meaningful collaboration.
- Develop a system for professional collaboration that includes an administrator's authentic participation on each team.
- Reward teachers for risk taking in analyzing their data and student evidence in a safe, respected collaborative team.
- Conduct objective evaluations of programs, professional learning, and collaborations on improved student-learning outcomes.
- Model the value of collaboration in your own professional improvement.
- Assure that professional learning includes modeling, practicing, and collaboration.

PRACTICAL STEPS FOR TEACHERS

- Collaborate to improve student-learning outcomes.
- Encourage your collaborative team to practice the characteristics of high-performing teams.
- Develop classroom action research to quantify improvements in your practice.
- Investigate developing a lesson-study research team.
- Develop agreements for collaborations that assure respect for one another and respect for time limits.

USEFUL ACADEMIC LANGUAGE

Collaboration—Direct interaction among at least two colleagues to make decisions related to a common goal.

Professional learning—Experiences that assist improvement in professional knowledge and expertise for greater effectiveness.

Reflection—Thinking about one's professional work, its effectiveness, and ways to improve. What is working for which students, under what conditions?

Additional Resources

Baines, L., & Fisher, J. (2013). Teaching challenging texts: Fiction, non-fiction, and multimedia. Lanham, MD: Rowman & Littlefield, Education Division.

Bonner, E. P. (2010). *Unearthing culturally responsive mathematics teaching.* Lanham, MD: Rowman & Littlefield, Education Division.

Fawcett, G. (2013). *Vocabulary in action.* Lanham, MD: Rowman & Littlefield, Education Division.

Garmston, R. J., & Wellman, B. M. (2013). *The adaptive school: A sourcebook for developing collaborative groups, 2nd edition.* Lanham, MD: Rowman & Littlefield, Education Division.

Glazer, S. M. (2013). *Words matter: Teacher language and student learning.* Lanham, MD: Rowman & Littlefield, Education Division.

Gray, G., & Donnelly, J. (2014). *History repeats itself in the classroom, too!: Prior knowledge and implementing the Common Core State Standards.* Lanham, MD: Rowman & Littlefield, Education Division.

Harris, A. S., Bruster, B. Peterson, B., & Shutt, T. (2010). *Examining and facilitating reflection to improve professional practice.* Lanham, MD: Rowman & Littlefield, Education Division.

Manville, M. (2014). *Common Core State Standards for grades K–1: Language arts instructional strategies and activities.* Lanham, MD: Rowman & Littlefield, Education Division.

Manville, M. (2014). *Common Core State Standards for grades 2–3: Language arts instructional strategies and activities.* Lanham, MD: Rowman & Littlefield, Education Division.

Manville, M. (2014). *Common Core State Standards for grades 4–5: Language arts instructional strategies and activities.* Lanham, MD: Rowman & Littlefield, Education Division.

Nelson-Reyes, A. M. (2013). *Success in school and career: Common core standards in language arts K–5.* Lanham, MD: Rowman & Littlefield, Education Division.

Porton, H. D. (2014). *Closing the gap between risk and resilience: How struggling learners can cope with Common Core State Standards.* Lanham, MD: Rowman & Littlefield, Education Division.

Roseboro, A. J. S. (2013). *Teaching reading in the middle school: Common core and more.* Lanham, MD: Rowman & Littlefield, Education Division.

Roseboro, A. J. S. (2013). *Teaching writing in the middle school: Common core and more.* Lanham, MD: Rowman & Littlefield, Education Division.

References

Addy, S., Englehardt, W., & Skinner, C. (January 2013). Basic facts about low-income children: Children under 18 years, 2011. New York: National Center for Children in Poverty. Retrieved February 1, 2014 from http://www.nccp.org/publications/pub_1074.html

Allen, R. (2012). *Education update: Support struggling students with academic rigor.* Alexandria, VA: Association for Supervision and Curriculum Development.

Bloom, B. S. (Ed.), Englehart, M. D., Hill, W. H., & Krathwohl, D. R. (1956). *Taxonomy of educational objectives, handbook I: The cognitive domain.* New York: David McKay.

Branch, G. F., Hanushek, E. A., & Rivkin, S. G. (Winter 2013). *School leaders matter,* 62–69. Educationnext.org.

Bransford, J. D., Brown, A. L., & Cocking, R. R. (Eds.). (2000). *How people learn* (expanded ed.). Washington, DC: National Academy Press.

Brunn, P. (2010). *The lesson planning handbook: Essential strategies that inspire student thinking and learning.* New York, NY: Scholastic.

Calkins, L., Ehrenworth, M., & Lehman, C. (2012). *Pathways to the common core: Accelerating achievement.* Portsmouth, NH: Heinemann.

Coleman, D. & Pimentel, S. (2011). *Publishers' criteria for the common core state standards in English language arts and literacy, grades 3–12.*www.sde.ct.gov/sde/cwp/view.asp?a=322592

Collier, V.P., & Thomas, W.P. (2004). The astounding effectiveness of dual language education for all. *NABE Journal of Research and Practice, 2*(1), 1–20.

Common Core State Standards Initiative (2010). *Supplemental information for Appendix A of Common Core State Standards for English language arts and literacy: New research on text complexity.* Washington, DC: National Governors Association, Council of Chief State School Officers.

Cummins, J. (2013). English language learners in the era of Common Core State Standards. Retrieved September 2, 2013 from the ESOL TAPESTRY website: http://tapestry.usf.edu/Cummins/index.html

Cummins, J. (1984). *Bilingualism and special education: Issues in assessment and pedagogy.* Clevedon, England: Multilingual Matters.

Dempster, F. N. (1997). Distributing and managing the conditions of encoding and practice. In E. L. Bjork & R. A. Bjork (Eds.). *Human memory* (pp. 197–236). San Diego, CA: Academic Press.

DiGisi, L., Parker, C., & Shaw, K. (August–September, 2013). Collaboration by state education departments produces free online ELA resources. *Reading Today, 31*(1), 24–26.

Dixon, L. Q., Zhao, J, Shin, J. Wu, S., Su, J, Burgess-Brigham, R., Gezer, M. U, & Snow, C. (March 2012). What we know about second language acquisition: A synthesis from four perspectives. *Review of Educational Research, 82*(1), 5–60.

Ellis, R. (2008). *The study of second language acquisition*. Oxford: Oxford University Press.

Fang, Z., & Pace, B. G. (October 2013). Teaching with challenging texts in the disciplines: Text complexity and close reading. *57*(2), 104–108.

Fiedler, R. (Summer 2012). ELA standards raise the bar on text complexity. *Changing schools*. Aurora, CO: Mc Rel.

Fisher, D., & Frey, N. (2008). *Better learning through structured teaching: A framework for the gradual release of responsibility*. Alexandria, VA: Association for Supervision and Curriculum Development.

Friend, M., Cook, L., Hurley-Chamberlin, D., & Shamberger, C. (2010). Co-teaching: An illustration of the complexity of collaboration in special education. *Journal of Educational and Psychological Consultation, 20*, 9–27.

Gallagher, K. S., Goodyear, R., Brewer, D. J., & Rueda, R. (2012). *Urban education: A model for leadership and policy*. New York, NY: Routledge.

Gamson, D. A., Lu, X., & Eckert, S. A. (2013). Challenging the research base of the common core state standards: A historical reanalysis of text complexity. *Educational Researcher, 42*(7), 381–391.

Glenberg, A. M., & Kaschak, M. (2002). Grounding language in action. *Psychonomic Bulletin & Review, 9*, 558–565.

Grissom, J. A., Loeb, S., & Master, B. (2013). Effective instructional time use for school leaders: Longitudinal evidence from observations of principals. *Educational Research, 42*(8), 433–444.

Hattie, J. (2009). *Visible learning: A synthesis of over 800 meta-analyses relating to achievement*. London, UK: Routledge.

Hess, K., Carlock, D., Jones, B., & Walkup, J. R. (2009). What exactly do fewer, clearer, and higher standards really look like in the classroom? Using the cognitive rigor matrix to analyze curriculum, plan lessons and implement assessments. Unpublished paper.

Hiebert, E. H. (2012). 7 Actions that teachers can take right now: Text complexity. Retrieved October 11, 2013 from http://textproject.org/professional-development/text-matters/7-actions-that-teachers-can-take-right-now-text-complexity/

Hiebert, E. H., & Mesmer, H. A. E. (January 2013). Meeting standard 10: Reading complex text. *Principal Leadership. 12*(5), 30–33.

Hunter, M. (1984). Knowing, teaching, and supervising. In P. Hosford (Ed.) *Using what we know about teaching* (pp. 169–92). Alexandria, VA: Association for Supervision and Curriculum Development.

Jensen, E. (1998). *Teaching with the brain in mind*. Alexandria, VA: Association for Supervision and Curriculum Development.

Koedinger, K. R., Corbett, A. T., & Perfetti, C. (2012). The knowledge-learning-instruction framework: Bridging the science-practice chasm to enhance robust student learning. *Cognitive Science: A Multidisciplinary Journal. 36*, 757–798.

Llewellyn, D. 2013. *Teaching high school science through inquiry and argumentation*. 2nd ed. Thousand Oaks, CA: Corwin Press.

Marzano, R. J. (2007). *The art and science of teaching*. Alexandria, VA: Association for Supervision and Curriculum Development.

Marzano, R. J. (2006). *Classroom assessment and grading that work*. Alexandria, VA: Association for Supervision and Curriculum Development.

Marzano, R. J., Pickering, D. J., & Pollock, J. E. (2001). *Classroom instruction that works: Research-based strategies for increasing student achievement*. Alexandria, VA: Association for Supervision and Curriculum Development.

Mayer, R. E. (November 2008). Applying the science of learning: Evidence-based principles for the design of multimedia instruction. *American Psychologist*, 760–769.

National Governor's Association Center for Best Practices & Council of Chief State School Officers. (2010). *Common Core State Standards for English, language arts and literacy in history/social studies, science and technical subjects: Appendix A.* Washington, DC: Authors.

(No author). (2013). Oak Ridge High School Literacy System. Orlando, Florida.

OECD (2010). *PISA 2009 results: What students know and can do—Student performance in reading, mathematics, and science.* (1). http://dx.doi.org/10.1787/9789264091450-en

Pahler, H., Cepeda, J. T., Wixted, J. T., & Rohrer, D. (2005). When does feedback facilitate learning of words? *Journal of Experimental Psychology: Learning, Memory, & Cognition, 31,* 3–8.

Puig, E. A., & Froelich, K. S. (2011). *The literacy coach: Guiding in the right direction,* 2ed. Boston, MA: Allyn & Bacon/Pearson.

Robelen, E. W. (December 11, 2013). U.S. math, science achievement exceeds world average. *Education Week,* 1–3.

Roediger, H. L. III., & Karpicke, J. D. (2006). The power of testing memory: Basic research and implications for educational practice. *Psychological Science, 1,* 181–210.

Skloot, R. (2010). *The immortal life of Henrietta Lacks.* New York, NY: Broadway Books.

Taylor, R. T., & Watson, R. (October 2013), Raising rigor for struggling students. *Principal Leadership, 14*(2), 56–59.

Taylor, R. T. (2010). *Leading learning: Change student achievement today!* Thousand Oaks, CA: Corwin Press.

Taylor, R. T. (2007). *Improving reading, writing, and content learning for students in grades 4–12.* Thousand Oaks, CA: Corwin Press.

Taylor, R. T., & Gunter, G. A. (2006). *The literacy leadership fieldbook.* Thousand Oaks, CA: Corwin Press.

US Department of Education, Institute of Education Sciences, National Center for Education Statistics. (2012). *The nation's report card: Reading 2011* (NCES Publication No. 2012-457). Retrieved from http://nces.ed.gov/nationsreportcard/pdf/main2011/2012457.pdf

US produces more high-performing students than any other nation. (October 2013). *NewsLeader, 61*(2), 1. Reston, VA: National Association of Secondary School Principals.

Webb, N. L. (2005). Webb alignment tool. Center for Educational Research University of Wisconsin-Madison.

www.Literacydesigncollaborative.org/

www.PARCConline.org/

www.smarterbalanced.org/

Index

106

Index

cognates, 30

cognitive complexity, 37, 46

cognitive engagement, 42

Cognitive Rigor Matrix, 37

collaboration, 10, 85; academic language for, 97; characteristics of, 85–87; as classroom factor, 65–66; with data and evidence, 91; leadership for, 94–95; on mini-assessments, 88–91; mutual goals and, 86–87; parity among participants, 86; practical steps for leaders, 96; practical steps for teachers, 97; professional learning and, 92–94; responsibility in, 87; shared accountability and, 87; sharing resources and, 87; student-learning outcomes and, 88–91, 95–96; as voluntary, 86

collaborative groups, 17, 18

collaborative planning, 5, 40; instructional, 88

college entrance exam preparation, 64

Collier, Virginia, 48

communication, precision in, 27

comprehension, 35, 56

connection, 43

Cook, Lynne, 85, 86, 87

Corbett, A. T., 74

Cornell notes daily summaries, 20

Council of Chief State School Officers (CCSSO), 1–2

culture: of active caring, 94; considerations for ELs, 57–58; of school, 62–63

Cummins, Jim, 48

data analysis, 88–91, 92

data study, 92

Depth of Knowledge (DOK), 37, 46

dictionaries, 30

differentiation, 18, 19, 58, 80–82; for ELE, 82; for ELs, 50, 82

digital resources, 4, 20, 64, 78; text complexity and, 39; for vocabulary instruction, 31

discipline-specific academic language, 27–28

DOK. *See* Depth of Knowledge

Douglass, Frederick, 52, 54

dual-language education programs, 54

Eckert, S. A., xiii

educational objectives, 35

effect sizes, 71, 83

ELA. *See* English Language Arts

ELD. *See* English language development

electronic assessments, 4

ELPD. *See* English Language Proficiency Development

ELs. *See* English learners

engagement, xiv, 23; cognitive, 42; research-based instruction and, 17–18

English for speakers of other languages (ESOL), 86

English Language Arts (ELA), 2, 27, 28, 48, 73

English language development (ELD), 49, 57

English Language Proficiency Development (ELPD), 59

English learners (ELs), 6, 22, 25, 28, 29, 39, 47–48; academic language, 60; advanced, 53, 55–57; beginning, 52–54; beyond beginning, 54–55; cultural considerations for, 57–58; differentiation for, 50, 82; intermediate, 55–57; learning scales for, 58–60; mutual goals and, 86; practical steps for leaders, 60; practical steps for teachers, 60; proficiency levels for, 49–50; something more and, 48–49; WIDA language proficiency levels and, 50–55

equity, 90

ESE. *See* exceptional student education

ESOL. *See* English for speakers of other languages

evaluation, 36–37

excellence, access to, 63, 90

exceptional student education (ESE), 82

exit slips, 20

expected language-acquisition outcomes, 32

extended thinking, 37

Farewell Address (Washington), 55

feedback, 71–72; generative, 15, 22, 23; implementation for, 76–80; to improve

improve learning, 20–23; practical steps for leaders, 23; practical steps for teachers, 23; scaffolding and, 10–17; teacher-led small-group instruction, 18–19

research-based vocabulary instruction, 28–31; instructional strategies, 30–31; vocabulary instruction protocol, 29–30

resilience, 67–68

resources: academic, 64; sharing of, 87. *See also* digital resources; under-resourced students

responsibilities: in collaboration, 87; of teachers and leaders, 68

rewards and sanctions, 63

rigor, 35; academic goals, 44; academic language for, 46; close reading, 40–41; cognitive complexity, 37; DOK, 37; levels of thinking, 35–37; motivation of students, 41–43; practical steps for leaders, 45; practical steps for teachers, 46; text complexity, 37–40; writing as thinking, 44–45

rotations, 19

sanctions, 63

SAT. *See* Scholastic Assessment Test

SBAC. *See* Smarter Balanced Assessment Consortium

scaffolding, 5, 9, 10–17, 23, 52, 66; assessment in, 15; guided practice, 13–14; independent practice, 14–15; instruction model for, 12; lesson introduction, 11–13; sample science instructional plan, 16, 16–17

scales, 83; for learning, 58–60, 72; planned, 78; printed, 78; quadratic, 80, 81; student-friendly, 75–76. *See also* Benchmark Scale with Evidence

Scholastic Assessment Test (SAT), 26, 51

school culture, 62–63

school factors, 62–64; academic resources, 64; rewards and sanctions, 63; school culture, 62–63

self-esteem, 67–68

self-monitoring, 71–72; implementation for, 76–80

sentence starters, 45

Shakespeare, William, 38

shared accountability, 87

skill or concept, 37

small-group instruction, 58; teacher-led, 18–19

Smarter Balanced Assessment Consortium (SBAC), 2, 3

standards-based learning target, 43

stations, 19

strategic thinking, 37

student-friendly scales, 75–76

student-learning outcomes, 88–91; collaborative instructional planning and, 88; leading, teaching, and coaching for, 95–96

student-owned literacy strategies, 10

success criteria, 83

synonyms, 31

teacher-led small-group instruction, 18–19

teachers: classroom factors controlled by, 64–68; effectiveness of, xiv; practical steps for, 6–7, 23, 32, 46, 60, 69, 83, 97; responsibilities of, 68

Tebow, Tim, 15

technology-enhanced instruction, 58

text complexity, 37–40, 46; effective use of, 40; misconceptions of, 39–40

text features, 11, 12

textual evidence, 56

thinking: extended, 37; higher-level, 4, 10; levels of, 35–37, 46; strategic, 37; writing as, 44–45

Thomas, Wayne, 48

thumbs up, 19

timeframes, for guided practice, 14

TIMSS. *See* Trend in Mathematics and Science Study

Tim Tebow effect, 15

Trend in Mathematics and Science Study (TIMSS), xiv

Turner, Fred, 78

under-resourced students, 6, 61–62; academic language for, 69; classroom factors and, 64–68; practical steps for leaders, 68–69; practical steps for teachers, 69; responsibilities of teachers and leaders, 68; school factors and, 62–64

About the Authors

Rosemarye T. Taylor

For more than 40 years, Rosemarye Taylor has distinguished herself as a scholarly practicing administrator and more recently as a Professor of Educational Leadership at the University of Central Florida in Orlando. Through her relationships with teachers and leaders she contributes to the in context improvement of teacher and leader effectiveness. She has published six books (such as *Improving Reading, Writing and Content Learning in Grades 4 and Up* and *Leading Learning: Change Student Achievement Today!*) and numerous articles on instructional leadership and learning. Regularly, she consults with principals, school district administrators, and educational institutions.

Rebecca Watson

For the past 15 years, Rebecca Watson has taught at the elementary and secondary levels, and been an instructional manager at the school district level in Orange County Public Schools, Florida. Her current work is as a school district administrator who primarily works with struggling and at-risk schools, teachers, and students to improve student achievement in her large urban school district. As a keynote speaker on the topic of working with students from poverty she is in demand. She recently published Raising Rigor for Struggling Readers in *Principal Leadership* (2013).

Joyce W. Nutta

Joyce Nutta is Professor of English for Speakers of Other Languages (ESOL) Education and the World Languages Education Program and TESOL PhD Track Coordinator at the University of Central Florida. Her research interests include the integration of English learner issues into teacher-preparation curricula, the use of technology to teach second languages, and technology-enhanced instruction in teacher preparation. Her research has been published in *Hispania, Foreign Language Annals, TESOL Journal,* and *CALICO Journal,* among other publications, and she is coeditor of *The Tapestry Journal: An International Multidisciplinary Journal on English Language Learner Education.* Her recent book, *Preparing Every Teacher to Reach English Learners: A Practical Guide for Teacher Educators,* received the American Association of Colleges for Teacher Education (AACTE) National Book Award for 2013, and the follow-up book for teachers and teacher candidates, *Educating English Learners: What Every Classroom Teacher Needs to Know,* will be published in the summer of 2014.

CPSIA information can be obtained at www.ICGtesting.com
Printed in the USA
BVOW05s2256300614

357812BV00003B/3/P